We dedicate this book to Mick Scott, husband,
best friend, sounding board and supporter,
of our dearest friend Gill Scott.

Acknowledgements

We very much appreciate bequests to CPAG in Scotland and Poverty Alliance from the estate of Robina Goodlad that have helped meet the costs of publishing this book. Robina provided active practical support to groups and organisations fighting poverty in both her personal and professional life. We hope that this publication will help contribute to creating a more socially just Scotland to which we and Robina are committed.

We are very grateful to all the people who contributed to this book. Their enthusiasm for tackling poverty and highlighting the major issues that must be addressed in Scotland at the current time was much appreciated.

For information and advice we would like to thank Jan Law, Elizabeth Mooney, Judith Paterson and Paul Dornan.

Finally, the editors would like to thank colleagues in Glasgow Caledonian University, the Poverty Alliance, Child Poverty Action Group and the Open University for their support.

CPAG promotes action for the prevention and relief of poverty among children and families with children. To achieve this, CPAG aims to raise awareness of the causes, extent, nature and impact of poverty, and strategies for its eradication and prevention; bring about positive policy changes for families with children in poverty; and enable those eligible for income maintenance to have access to their full entitlement. If you are not already supporting us, please consider making a donation, or ask for details of our membership schemes and publications.

Published by CPAG, in assocation with
Scottish Poverty Information Unit and Poverty Alliance
94 White Lion Street, London N1 9PF

The views expressed in this book are the authors' and do not necessarily express those of CPAG.

A CIP record for this book is available from the British Library

IBSN 978 1 901698 97 8

Cover and design by Devious Designs (based on an original design by John Gahagan) 0114 275 5634
Typeset by Boldface 020 7833 8868
Printed by Russell Press 0115 978 4505
Cover photos © Howard Davies/Reportdigital; Jess Hurd/Reportdigital

Contents

About the organisations

Child Poverty Action Group in Scotland is part of CPAG and works to promote action for the relief, directly or indirectly, of poverty among children and families with children. We work to ensure that those on low incomes get their full entitlement to welfare benefits and tax credits. In our campaigning and information work we seek to improve benefits and policies for low-income families in order to eradicate the injustice of poverty. If you are not already supporting us, please consider making a donation, or ask for details of membership schemes and publications. For further information, please visit www.cpag.org.uk/scotland

With over 14,000 students across Scotland, **The Open University** is Scotland's leading provider of part-time higher education. We are committed to widening access to higher education and have an open admissions policy and, as a result, no previous qualifications are necessary to study at degree level. One in five Open University students in Scotland is on a low income or is unemployed. They are able to study because they receive a financial award which entitles them to a free place. For further information contact The Open University in Scotland on 0131 226 3851, scotland@open.ac.uk, or visit www.open.ac.uk/scotland

The Poverty Alliance is the national anti-poverty network in Scotland and was set up in 1992. It works with a range of community, voluntary and statutory organisations to find better solutions to the problems of poverty in Scotland. The Alliance attempts to influence anti-poverty policy by lobbying and campaigning, organising seminars and conferences, producing briefing papers and other information. A key goal for the Alliance is to have the voices of people experiencing poverty heard in policy processes. To do this we work with a number of partners across the UK and Europe and represent the UK Coalition Against Poverty and the European Anti-Poverty Network in Scotland. For further information on our work please visit: www.povertyalliance.org

The Scottish Poverty Information Unit is based at Glasgow Caledonian University. The Unit provides information on poverty to those working in the anti-poverty field, in order to enable them to combat poverty more effectively. Research, consultancy, conference organisation and publication are the key activities of the Unit. The Unit is committed to working in partnership to tackle poverty in Scotland. For further information on our work please visit: www.scottishpovertyinformation.org

About the contributors

Lynn Burnett is Policy Officer at The Poverty Alliance.

Professor Christine Cooper is Head of Accounting and Finance at the University of Strathclyde.

Professor Mike Danson is Professor of Scottish and Regional Economics at the University of Paisley.

Marion Davis is Senior Manager of Policy Services at One Plus.

John Dickie is Head of the Child Poverty Action Group in Scotland.

Mick Doyle is Community Development Team Leader at the Scottish Refugee Council. Mick is writing in a personal capacity.

Fiona Forsyth is Director of Rosemount Lifelong Learning.

Tesfu Gessesse is Director of the Black Community Development Project.

Morag Gillespie is Research Fellow at the Scottish Poverty Information Unit.

Elspeth Gracey is Practice Development Manager at the Community Health Exchange.

Mhoraig Green is a Research Fellow at The Poverty Alliance.

Peter Kelly is Director of The Poverty Alliance.

David Liddell is Director of the Scottish Drugs Forum.

Dr John H McKendrick is Senior Lecturer, Human Geography at the School of Law and Social Sciences, Glasgow Caledonian University and is a senior researcher within the Scottish Poverty Information Unit.

Dr Gerry Mooney is Senior Lecturer in Social Policy/Staff Tutor at The Open University in Scotland.

Janet Muir is Manager of Community Health Exchange.

Dr Stephen Sinclair is Research Fellow at the School of Law and Social Sciences, Glasgow Caledonian University and Scottish Poverty Information Unit.

Robin Tennant is Fieldwork Manager at The Poverty Alliance.

Geoff Whittam is a Reader at the University of Paisley.

Section One
Introduction

One

Poverty and anti-poverty policy: continuity and change

Gerry Mooney

Poverty in Scotland 2007 is the fifth in a series of books, which, since the mid-1990s, have provided a comprehensive picture of the extent of poverty in Scottish society. Each of these books has been charged with making accessible what is often a complex world of figures, diverse measurements, competing definitions and contrasting interpretations of poverty – and identifying what should be done to address poverty. Since the publication of the first edition of this book in 1995,[1] much has changed in relation to poverty – and in particular with regard to anti-poverty policy. The last edition of this series, *Poverty in Scotland 2002: people, places and policies*,[2] which focused on poverty in the early years of Scottish devolution, was concerned to offer more detailed discussions than earlier editions of different dimensions of poverty and government strategies. In this edition we follow suit, by offering a series of essays that provide reflections from people working in the field of poverty action and research (not necessarily the editors' views). These build upon our detailed examination of the main patterns of poverty as they feature in Scotland in the first decade of the twenty-first century.

This book has largely been written and produced in the second half of 2006. By the time it is published, the campaigns for the third Scottish Parliament elections in May 2007 will be well under way. It is the hope of all who have contributed to this collection that the issue of poverty will feature prominently in the campaign, with this book playing a part in helping to encourage (and provoke!) debate and argument over anti-poverty policies.

Devolution and the policy-making contexts

There is little doubt that governments across the UK have been very active across a wide range of social and welfare policy areas since the mid- to late-1990s. From the outset we need to be aware that we are now living in a context of multi-government: UK/Westminster, Scotland/Holyrood, Europe and local government. It no longer makes sense to talk of a government approach to policy but more appropriately to speak of the actions of different governments and levels of government.

While the focus of this volume is on poverty and poverty policy in Scotland, clearly we cannot ignore the UK dimension. The main reason for this is that the devolution 'settlement' of 1998 'reserved' to the UK parliament in Westminster a range of policy-making areas which have UK-wide consequences. For the purposes of this book the most important of these include social security, aspects of employment policy, economic and fiscal policies and, an issue of increasing importance, citizenship policy. This last category encompasses all aspects of asylum and immigration policy making. One of the key underpinning themes of this collection is that poverty and disadvantage cannot adequately be considered as issues that 'belong' exclusively to a particular range of policy-making areas. Clearly, social security legislation and employment policies will, together with taxation and fiscal policy, have a major impact on the levels and experience of poverty across the UK today. But in other ways, perhaps at first glance more difficult ways to comprehend, immigration policies, family policies, education policies, sustainability, industrial relations and so on, all have important consequences for those who are poor, disadvantaged and socially excluded across the UK today. Some of these policy areas are featured in Section Three.

That this is the fifth in the *Poverty in Scotland* series in part illustrates the point that poverty is a pervasive social problem in Scottish society. We do not have to look far to see the different and multiple ways in which poverty continues to plague a sizeable proportion of the population. Poor educational attainment rates, low wages, inadequate housing, homelessness and patterns of criminality are often directly or indirectly related to poverty in some shape or form.[3]

There are many different ways of understanding and explaining poverty, each of which carries particular ideas about the underlying causes of poverty and how these should be addressed. The thinking that shaped the main policies of New Labour from 1997 included a rejection of the previous approaches of both the Conservatives in the 1970s and 1980s as well as previous Labour Governments. Instead, New Labour committed itself to the development of a more 'pragmatic' approach that involved the promotion of new ways of working between departments; and the adoption of evidence-based policy development. New Labour's strategy in relation to poverty has been one which stresses that the 'old certainties' about social protection and the welfare state no longer hold the key to successful policy development. A pragmatic approach, focusing on policies and solutions (regardless of their position in the political spectrum) that would address the problems the country faced and improve people's lives was now heralded as the priority for government. Often referred to as a 'Third Way' approach, this is underpinned by the argument that both the 'tax and spend', nationalising and state interventionist policies of 'old' Labour, as well as the market-driven policies of the Conservatives, failed to tackle poverty and disadvantage in Britain. Against these 'two failed pasts', New Labour sought to construct an approach that drew on new ideas and ways of working which it claimed were more in tune with recent economic and social developments, both in Britain and internationally. The key social and economic changes highlighted included: reconfigurations in family structure; shifting population (or demographic) trends – in particular the ageing of the population; 'globalisation'; and the importance of transforming Britain into a 'lean' and efficient knowledge-based economy, with a 'flexible', well-educated and highly skilled workforce. Importantly for this book, 'reforming' the welfare state and 'modernising' public services were also regarded by New Labour as key to this 'renewal' of the British economy and society.

Although the 'modernising' drive of New Labour was more pragmatic than ideological, several important values have shaped New Labour policies in relation to poverty. These include the belief that 'social exclusion' rather than solely income or material poverty should be addressed; a belief that any strategy should be directed at those who were willing to help themselves; and finally a belief that there were 'anti-social' values held by some families and communities that prevented anti-poverty strategies working effectively. These values are reflected in policies that seek to influence and shape the behaviours of those considered to be socially excluded, emphasising responsibilities and duties more than rights.

Governments in both Edinburgh and London recognise that income poverty continues to be a 'problem' today. But this is increasingly couched in an understanding of disadvantage as being 'wider' and more 'multi-dimensional'. The Government has therefore championed the notion of 'social exclusion'.[4] While this notion has a relatively short history in the UK context, it has a longer pedigree in Europe where it has been developed and adopted by the European Union over several decades. It is constructed as representing a 'more dynamic' and wide-ranging definition of the relationships involved in poverty. There is an implicit promise in the notion of social exclusion to examine all of the processes contributing to poverty, including, for example, racism and sexism and other forms of discrimination. However, as some critics point out, the term raises questions of 'who includes whom and on what terms? And with regards to exactly what are they to be included?' For example, the UK Government and the Scottish Executive have made it clear that their primary concerns are with social exclusion and poverty, not inequality. Policies have been aimed at increasing equality of opportunities, *not* equality of outcome.[5] The main goal for the Government was to create a system which would ensure 'work for those who can and security for those who cannot' and that the long-term effects of poverty would not prevent new generations or areas becoming socially excluded. Whilst this shows that the Government implicitly accepted the existence of income poverty, it also indicated that issues of disadvantage were felt to be wider, though not 'wide' enough to be seriously challenged through an attack on the causes of inequality. The use of the concept 'social exclusion' has been promoted as a way of targeting policy towards work as the best route out of poverty, as well as directing policy in a more targeted way towards families and communities rather than society as a whole.

The concept of social exclusion rather than social inequality, then, informs New Labour's and the Labour-LibDem coalition in Scotland's idea of anti-poverty policy. However, as has been widely argued, in the hands of New Labour, social exclusion is a term that is overwhelmingly constructed and understood as exclusion from work – defined as paid employment – and, in turn, social inclusion is principally dependent upon entering paid employment. This language has grown out of a different, but related, set of values to that utilised by the Conservatives. The impact on policy was that the welfare state came to be seen increasingly as a tool through which the social inclusion of the poorest individuals and groups in society could be achieved by supporting people to enter the world of paid work.

The debate about the future of welfare in Britain, and in this poverty policy occupies a key position, has also become increasingly focused on morality, behaviour and personal character. In important respects, recent welfare 'reforms' have been as much about forging fundamental changes in the relationship between the individual and the state, as they have been about developing new ways of tackling poverty or social exclusion. The language of, and stress upon, 'responsibilities' and 'duties' has come to be a consistent feature of many social and welfare policies. In turn, this is linked to the idea of the 'greater good', that individuals have important duties to family, community and to society as a whole. For those who are defined as 'side-stepping' their social responsibilities, an increasing range of penalties have developed as in, for example, the withdrawal of benefits for those neglecting to take up work. Welfare to work, and the increasing emphasis on work-related benefits, is at the core of the entire New Labour approach to poverty as social exclusion.

It is already apparent that in discussing poverty in any meaningful or adequate way we are immediately drawn into a wider range of issues about the structure of society, of the role of the individual, the state and so on. Importantly, we are also drawn into issues of inequality. There is a complex inter-relationship between poverty and inequality – but to grasp this fully means that we recognise that these are not the same thing. It is possible to have inequality and no poverty. By contrast, poverty cannot exist without some degree of inequality.

Devolution and 'Scottish solutions'

Devolution in 1999 was generally welcomed as allowing the development of distinctively 'Scottish solutions for Scottish problems'.[6] To quote Donald Dewar, then Secretary of State for Scotland:[7]

> We have a proud tradition in Scotland of working to tackle social division. We have developed innovative responses to social problems, many of which are now being promoted within the UK as models of good practice. We have a body of people... who are committed to creating a fairer society in Scotland. And in the not too distant future we will have a Scottish Parliament, which will give us the opportunity to develop Scottish solutions to Scottish needs, and to bring the arm of government closer to the needs of the people. Devolution matters. It will let us take the decisions that matter here in Scotland. It is an end in itself: but it is a means to other ends, and none more important than the creation of a socially cohesive Scotland.

The idea of 'Scottish solutions' has become a popular phrase among leading Scottish ministers, not least in relation to social policy making.

The promotion of social justice, for example, has been a priority for the Scottish Executive since devolution. In *Social Justice: a Scotland where everyone matters*, the Scottish Executive first set out its wide-ranging social justice strategy, which was presented as 'the most comprehensive framework ever for tackling poverty in Scotland'.[8] This programme was founded on a 'life cycle approach' that focused on both people and places. Ten long-term targets were identified for achieving a more socially just Scotland. These targets included defeating child poverty within a generation (thereby reflecting the commitment given the previous year by Blair and New Labour at Westminster), ensuring that every 19-year-old was in education, training or work; full employment; and reducing inequalities between different communities across Scotland. The targets were supplemented by 29 'milestones', which would be measured annually to show how far progress had been made in meeting the long-term targets. A Social Justice Annual Report was to be published detailing progress.[9]

After the second Holyrood Parliament elections in 2003, the Social Justice Strategy was reviewed and the outcome was a revised approach.[10] 'Social justice' was 'dropped' as the term describing anti-poverty policy, and was replaced by the more New Labour-sounding *Closing the Opportunity Gap*. This had three broad aims: to prevent individuals or families from falling into poverty; to provide pathways out of poverty; and to sustain individuals or families in a lifestyle free from poverty. In December 2004, six objectives were identified:

1. To increase the chances of sustained employment for vulnerable and disadvantaged groups – in order to lift them out of poverty permanently.
2. To improve the confidence and skills of the most disadvantaged children and young people – in order to provide them with the greatest chance of avoiding poverty post-school.
3. To reduce the vulnerability of low-income families to financial exclusion and multiple debt – in order to prevent them becoming over-indebted and/or to lift them out of poverty
4. To regenerate the most deprived neighbourhoods – in order that people living there can take advantage of job opportunities and improve their quality of life.
5. To increase the rate of improvement of the health status of people living in the most deprived communities – in order to improve their quality of life, including their employability prospects.

6. To improve access to high-quality services for the most disadvantaged groups and individuals in rural communities – in order to improve their quality of life and enhance their access to opportunity.

These six main objectives were underpinned by ten targets:

A **Reducing economic inactivity in the areas of highest economic inactivity**. (Number of workless people dependent on social security benefits in Glasgow, North and South Lanarkshire, Renfrewshire and Inverclyde, Dundee, and West Dunbartonshire by 2007 and by 2010.)

B **Reducing the proportion of 16–19-year-olds not in education, employment or training**. (By 2008.)

C **Public sector and large employers to tackle aspects of in-work poverty by providing employees with the opportunity to develop skills and progress in their career**. (NHS Scotland will set an example by providing 1,000 job opportunities, with support for training and progression once in post, between 2004 and 2006 to people who are currently economically inactive or unemployed.)

D **Tackling a significant aspect of health inequalities**. (Reduce health inequalities by increasing the rate of improvement for under-75 coronary heart disease mortality and under-75 cancer mortality (1995–2003) for the most deprived communities by 15 per cent by 2008.)

E **Providing an integrated package of support for the most vulnerable children**. (By 2008, ensure that children and young people who need it have an integrated package of appropriate health care and education support.)

F **Improving educational attainment at age 16 for the lowest attaining pupils across the country**. (Increase the average tariff score of the lowest attaining 20 per cent of S4 pupils by 5 per cent by 2008.)

G **Improving educational outcomes for looked-after children**. (By 2007 ensure that at least 50 per cent of all looked-after young people leaving care have entered education, employment or training.)

H **Improving access to high-quality services in rural areas**. (By 2008, improve service delivery in rural areas so that agreed improvements to accessibility and quality are achieved for key services in remote and disadvantaged communities.)

J **Tackling community regeneration by improving local infrastructure in the most disadvantaged communities**. (By 2008 in employability, education, health, access to local services, and quality of the local environment.)

K **Reducing the risk of financial exclusion and multiple debt for low-income families**. (By 2008 increase the availability of appropriate financial services and money advice to disadvantaged communities.)

These targets were selected because they were deemed to have the potential for the Scottish Executive to have the greatest impact on poverty in Scotland. While the high-level aims of *Closing the Opportunity Gap* are focused on poverty, we can see here that the more specific targets are largely focused on work (as paid employment) as the route out of poverty for this, and the next, generation. In all of this, therefore, there is little, really, that distinguishes Scottish anti-poverty/social justice policy from that of the rest of the UK (and in many respects it is similar to the Department for Work and Pensions' *Opportunities for All* programme).[11] Child poverty is foregrounded; work and enterprise are seen as essential elements of progress, while inequality is hardly mentioned, other than when it is deemed to undermine the pursuit of competitiveness.

While the 1999 social justice strategy, and now *Closing the Opportunity Gap*, represent the most visible aspects of the Scottish Executive's social justice strategy, other policies (for example, social housing policies, community planning partnerships, the equalities agenda, and the work of the Scottish Women's Budget Group) also include an explicit social justice element.

The structure of *Poverty in Scotland 2007*

A key goal of this book is to provide an accessible overview of poverty in contemporary Scotland. This is addressed in **Section Two: The nature of poverty in Scotland**. Here, we provide a detailed picture of poverty by bringing together a broad range of statistical information drawn from different sources to review which groups are more likely to face poverty (Chapter 4). However, in addition to the provision of *quantitative* data and information, Section Two also offers a more *qualitative* exploration of some of the key ways in which poverty shapes the lived, day-to-day experiences of a significant section of the Scottish population (Chapter 5). Furthermore, poverty cannot be fully grasped by focusing on statistical data alone and therefore Section Two also provides a discussion of some of the main factors that lead to poverty (Chapter 3), and a discussion of what we understand poverty to be (Chapter 2).

Following from *Poverty in Scotland 2002*, **Section Three: Combating poverty** offers informed short essays or 'opinion pieces' that consider particular areas of poverty and poverty policies. Here a key focus, as the subtitle of this section acknowledges, is on tackling poverty through the policy, practice and provision of services. Contributions to this section are drawn from across political, campaigning, voluntary and academic sectors. The authors of the essays have been asked to provide a brief overview of government policies in their respective topic area and to offer some critical reflections on their effectiveness or otherwise. **Section Four: Conclusions** considers the main themes and issues arising from the information presented in Section Two and from the essays that are featured in Section Three.

Finally, **Appendix One** provides a policy diary, which details many of the key anti-poverty legislation since 1997 and, in particular, since Scottish devolution in 1999. **Appendix Two** gives guidance to key data and information sources, and argues the case for improving the quality of information to better understand and tackle poverty in Scotland in the years ahead.

Notes

1 R Tennant, *Child and Family Poverty in Scotland: the facts*, Save the Children Scotland, 1995

2 U Brown, G Scott, G Mooney and B Duncan (eds), *Poverty in Scotland 2002: people, places and policies*, Child Poverty Action Group, 2002, available online at: http://www.povertyinformation.org/show.php?contentid=3

3 For more detailed discussions, see D Cook, *Criminal and Social Justice*, Sage, 2006; R Lister, *Poverty*, Polity Press, 2004; R Wilkinson, *The Impact of Inequality*, Routledge, 2005

4 R Levitas, *The Inclusive Society? Social exclusion and New Labour*, Palgrave Macmillan, 2006; G Mooney and C Johnstone, 'Scotland Divided: poverty, inequality and the Scottish Parliament', *Critical Social Policy*, Vol 63, pp155–182

5 B Jackson and P Segal*, Why Inequality Matters*, Catalyst, 2004

6 G Mooney and G Scott (eds), *Exploring Social Policy in the 'New' Scotland*, The Policy Press, 2005

7 Scottish Office Press Release, 3 November 1998

8 Scottish Executive, *Social Justice: a Scotland where everyone matters*, Scottish Executive, 1999, available online at: http://www.scotland.gov.uk/library2/doc07/sjmd-00.htm

9 Three such reports were published in 2000, 2001 and 2002. For more information, see http://www.scotland.gov.uk/Topics/People/Social-Inclusion/17415/milestones.

10 Scottish Executive, *Closing the Gap: Scottish budget for 2003-2006*, Scottish Executive, 2003, available online at: http://www.scotland.gov.uk/Publications/2002/10/15579/11898; Scottish Executive, *Closing the Opportunity Gap*, available online at: www.scotland.gov.uk/closingtheopportunitygap

11 Department for Work and Pensions, *Opportunity for All: eighth annual report*, The Stationery Office, 2006, available online at: http://www.dwp.gov.uk/ofa/reports/latest.asp

Section Two
The nature of poverty in Scotland

Two

Definitions, measurements and incidence of poverty

Peter Kelly and John H McKendrick

Key ideas

Attempts to explain the different approaches to defining and measuring poverty are often overly technical and theoretical, written by academics and statisticians for 'people like them'. However, the ways in which we conceptualise and define poverty have implications for the number of people that are counted as living in poverty; the understanding that society in general has about those living in poverty; and about the policy solutions that we develop to address the problem. Therefore, we must all be concerned about how poverty is defined and measured.

There is little doubt that ideas about poverty are complex, often contradictory and influenced by factors such as personal experiences, value judgements and belief systems. Consequently, definitions of poverty are also contested. There is no single, universally accepted, definition of poverty. In this opening section, we explain what we mean by poverty, and describe how it is related to ideas of inequality, social exclusion, social inclusion and social justice.

Poverty and inequality

Before looking at some of the main approaches to defining and measuring poverty, it is useful to say something about the relationship between poverty and inequality. There is a close relationship between these two concepts and all too often they appear to be used interchangeably, in particular when relative poverty is discussed. The issue of the gap between the richest and poorest in our society (inequality) is of fundamental concern, and many of the authors in this book make reference to the lack of progress in addressing this gap, but we are primarily focused on the character and experiences of those who do not have sufficient income (poverty).

Absolute and relative poverty

The two most common ways of conceptualising poverty are through the terms 'absolute' and 'relative' poverty.

Absolute poverty refers to the level of resources needed to sustain physical survival. People are poor if they cannot feed, clothe or house themselves and their dependants. This is a definition of poverty that is only about subsistence, the amount needed to keep body and soul together. As Ruth Lister points out, absolute definitions of poverty are closely linked to nutrition, whereby a person or family can be considered to be poor if they do not have sufficient resources to feed themselves.[1] This conception of poverty is one that is often viewed as a 'common sense' approach to defining poverty. Its use in relation to Scotland or the UK is often made in comparison to other parts of the world – 'there is real poverty in Malawi, but not here' – or in relation to other times – 'we used to have poverty in Scotland, but not any more'. This absolute definition of poverty shows that income is central to the way we conceptualise poverty, as poverty is not having enough income to buy life's necessities. However, the definition of 'necessity' must be based on some assessment of need and our understanding of what is an essential need varies over time and across place. For this reason few serious analysts, and none of the major political parties, would use an absolute measure to understand poverty in Scotland in the twenty-first century.

Relative poverty is defined in relation to the standards of living in a society at a particular time. People live in poverty when they are denied an income sufficient for their material needs, and when these circumstances exclude them from taking part in activities which are an accepted part of daily life in that society. One problem with this approach is that in an affluent society it could become difficult to distinguish between those who are poor and those who are just less well off; some commentators argue that relative definitions refer to inequality, not poverty.

Despite perceived shortcomings, in this book we use the relative measure of poverty, believing that poverty should be defined by the standards of society as it is today. By using a relative measure we arrive at a better understanding of poverty in the twenty-first century:

... an understanding based on a measure that has the lack of income at its heart, but which acknowledges that poverty is about what that lack of income implies – the inability to obtain the types of diet, participate in the activities and have the living conditions and amenities which are customary ... in the societies to which they [the poor] belong.[2]

Later in this chapter, we discuss how the *Households Below Average Income* data are used to calculate measures of absolute low income and relative low income.

Social inclusion and social exclusion

Definitions of social exclusion usually describe how and why it occurs, as well as its implications. The European Union (EU) notes that social exclusion occurs when people cannot fully participate or contribute to society because of '... the denial of civil, political, social, economic and cultural rights'.[3] Social exclusion is also viewed as resulting from combinations of linked problems, for example, unemployment, poor skills, low incomes, poor housing, bad health and family breakdown. The term is useful in encompassing the multi-dimensional nature of poverty, and examining the complex relationship between causes and effects of poverty.

The term social exclusion has been dominant in recent UK policy debates. However, in Scotland the phrase 'social inclusion' has been used more often, both by the Scottish Executive and by the voluntary sector. It could be argued that the use of 'social inclusion' suggests an approach that is more focused on the outcomes of policies, rather than the problems themselves – the overall aim of the policies being a more inclusive society. Such a distinction can be over-emphasised. For example, although the UK Government set up the Social Exclusion Unit (now the Social Exclusion Task Force within the Cabinet Office), it is also responsible for the publication of the *National Action Plan on Social Inclusion*.[4] It is possible to spend too much time considering the subtle differences in meaning between exclusion and inclusion; the important question is the content of the policies that governments pursue in order to tackle exclusion or promote inclusion.

Roll points out that a drawback of a very broad approach to social exclusion is that issues of deprivation and disadvantage are concealed within broader social questions.[5] Discrimination, for example, is a major cause of poverty but discrimination does not necessarily imply poverty;

many who face discrimination are not poor. For example, gay men encounter discrimination, but are under-represented among those living in poverty. Moreover, social exclusion is difficult both to measure and to evaluate.

In this book, we are primarily concerned with poverty and the policies that are developed to tackle it. However, policies to tackle poverty and social exclusion are intimately linked and we do not seek to separate anti-poverty policy from social inclusion policy. An understanding of social exclusion/inclusion adds to our understanding of poverty as a multi-dimensional phenomenon, with interlinked causes and solutions.

Social justice

Social justice is also a broad and contested term. Definitions vary across the political spectrum; they include ideas of distributive justice, utilitarianism, equality, and libertarian ideas of 'governance'. Fundamentally, to aim for social justice is to pursue the belief

> ... that society can be reshaped – its major social and political institutions changed – so that each person gets a fair share of the benefits, and carries a fair share of the responsibilities, of living together in a community.[6]

The Commission on Social Justice, set up in 1992 by the late John Smith, the leader of the Labour Party at that time, to carry out an independent enquiry into economic and social reform, noted: '...our view of social justice consists of four key ideas'. These were: equal worth of all citizens; citizens' entitlement to be able to meet their basic needs; the widest possible spread of opportunities; and the reduction or elimination of unjust inequalities.[7] Although the Scottish Executive uses the term social justice, it does not define it. It is used to cover the Executive's commitment to tackling poverty and disadvantage, rebuilding and strengthening our communities, and increasing opportunity for all through education.

Measurement of poverty

As noted at the start of this chapter, the way we calculate the number of people who live in poverty has become very technical and can be off-putting. The problem first arose partly due to the fact that there has never been an official measure of poverty in the UK. In response, organisations and individuals outside government who were concerned with tackling poverty began to use a variety of different methods to assess levels of poverty in Britain. As a consequence, there is now a mass of complex data available about the extent of poverty that is not always compatible, and can be difficult to interpret. Nevertheless, two commonly used measures emerged as the preferred ways of measuring the incidence of poverty – using *Households Below Average Income* data and using data on the recipients of welfare payments.

The situation is now complicated by the fact that in the UK there is a new official measure of *child* poverty, although there is still no official poverty line for the population as a whole. Thus, at this point in time, there are three main ways of measuring the incidence of poverty in Scotland.

Child poverty

In 1999, the UK Government committed itself to eradicate child poverty within a generation. The Scottish Executive shares this vision. The Department for Work and Pensions (DWP) consulted with users between 2002 and 2003, presenting four options for measuring child poverty: (1) using a small number of indicators (for example education and unemployment) to track low income; (2) construction of an index using specified indicators to produce an overall figure; (3) producing an overall figure that combines relative low income and material deprivation; (4) the use of a core set of indicators of low income and consistent poverty.[8]

Following this consultation, the DWP, in conjunction with HM Treasury, has devised a three-tier measure of child poverty, which consists of measures of absolute low income, relative low income, and material deprivation and low income combined (Table 2.1).[9] It was expected that data on the third tier – material deprivation and low income combined – would be published for the first time toward the end of 2006.

Households Below Average Income

Households Below Average Income (HBAI) is an annual review of income distribution compiled by the DWP (previously the Department of Social Security), first published in 1988. It is a major source of information on

Table 2.1:

UK government's new three-tier measure of child poverty

Tier 1: Absolute low income

Number and proportion of children in households whose equivalised income before housing costs is below 60 per cent of inflation adjusted GB median income in 1998/99. This is a measure of whether the poorest families are seeing their incomes rise in real terms.

Tier 2: Relative low income

Number and proportion of children in households whose equivalised income before housing costs is below 60 per cent of GB median income in the same year. This is a measure of whether the poorest families are keeping pace with the growth of incomes in the economy as a whole.

Tier 3: Material deprivation and low income combined

Number and proportion of children that are both materially deprived and in households whose equivalised income before housing costs is less than 70 per cent of the GB median in the current year. This is to provide a wider measure of children's living standards.

people living on low incomes and provides '... an explicitly relative measure which looks at how people at the bottom of the income distribution have fared in relation to the average'.[10]

HBAI provides official figures on low income. In the past, 50 per cent of *mean* net income was used as the income poverty measure. In 1998 the Statistical Program Committee of the European Union decided that 60 per cent of *median* income should be used as the measure of income poverty when making international comparisons.[11] This is now the favoured measure of the UK Government. It should be noted that the EU Committee also recommended that other thresholds (for example 40, 50 and 70 per cent of the median) should also be used when considering poverty, in order to obtain the fullest picture. The use of these thresholds is not widespread in the UK, but they can be helpful in understanding the severity or depth of low income.

Mean and median refer to different ways of measuring the average. Although the *mean* is most commonly used as the way of measuring an average, the favoured way of measuring poverty and low income is to use the median. Mean income is found by adding all the incomes of a population and dividing the result by the number of people in that population.

But the measure can be easily distorted by very low or very high income figures. The *median* refers to the mid-point of a given set of figures. The median measure of average income is less susceptible to distortions, in particular from those on high incomes, and is therefore more reliable.

It should be noted that although these measures are now widely used, the adequacy of these income thresholds as measures of poverty has not been established, so we do not know if the incomes they represent actually reflect the level at which people live in poverty.[12] It should always be remembered then that people with incomes above the thresholds are not necessarily living lives free of hardship.

There are further complications. Two measures are used in the HBAI series: net income *before* housing costs, and net income *after* housing costs. In this publication, the 'after housing cost' measure is used when comparing across government office regions and national regions, as housing costs represent a fixed budget item over which low-income families have little choice and there are marked variations in housing expenditure across the country. Discounting housing costs from calculations of low income ensures that we are better able to compare what low-income families across different regions have at their disposal to spend. However, it should be noted that a 'before housing costs' measure is used in the new official UK measure of child poverty.

The HBAI series also recognises that income levels must be adjusted if they are to be used as a measure of living standards. For example, a couple with four children will require a higher level of income to maintain the same standard of living as one adult living alone. This adjustment is known as equivalisation. The 2004/05 HBAI series uses the McClements equivalisation scale, although the 2005/06 HBAI series will switch to the OECD equivalisation scale. The new child poverty measure already uses the modified OECD equivalisation scale. Technical notes provide guidance on understanding how equivalisation works and the differences between equivalisation scales.[13] For now, it is enough to note that the modified OECD equivalisation scale gives more weight than the McClements equivalisation scale to 0–4-year-olds and to 14–15-year-olds. Clearly, for HBAI income data to be used as a measure of income-based poverty, it is first necessary to disaggregate data by family household types.

Table 2.2 shows four sets of information for different family household types. The second and third columns report the typical income in £/week for different family types in Great Britain (the mean and the median income – after housing costs and including the self-employed). The fourth and fifth columns report the 'poverty lines', that is the weekly income

Table 2.2:

Weekly income and income-based poverty lines (after housing costs and including the self-employed) in 2004/05 for different family household types, Great Britain

Family household type	Weekly income £		Weekly income-based poverty lines £	
	Mean	Median	50% mean	60% median
Single with no children	206	167	103	100
Couple with no children	375	304	188	183
Single with two children (aged 5 and 11)	383	311	191	186
Couple with two children (aged 5 and 11)	552	447	276	268

Source: Department for Work and Pensions, *Households Below Average Income, 2004/05*, Corporate Document Services, 2006, Table 2.3

Note: Poverty would be defined as an income at or below the figures listed in columns 4 and 5 of this table.

levels below which different family household types may be considered to be living in poverty (50 per cent of the mean income and 60 per cent of the median income – after housing costs and including the self-employed).

There is one final complicating, and at times confusing, issue which must be remembered when looking at HBAI figures. In the context of HBAI, the definitions of 'absolute' and 'relative' low incomes are very different from those outlined on page 14. Both refer to different income thresholds below which people are understood to be living in absolutely or relatively low-income households.

Absolute low income in relation to the HBAI figures refers to those households with less than 60 per cent of 1996/97 GB median income. This threshold is adjusted by inflation for each subsequent year. According to the DWP, absolute low income '... is important to measure whether the poorest families are seeing their incomes rise in real terms'.[14]

Relative low income in relation to the HBAI figures refers to the number and proportion of households with below 60 percent of GB median income for each year. The threshold is, therefore, recalculated every year to account for increases in median incomes, rather than simply being fixed for one year then increased by inflation. This measure allows us to consider whether those on low incomes are keeping up with the rest of society.

As the 'absolute' and 'relative' figures for low income are measured in different ways, it is necessary to be clear about what these figures may mean. It could be argued that the figures for 'absolute' low income are of less use when attempting to understand what is happening with low incomes. As incomes generally rise over time, even for those on low incomes, we would expect the proportion of people with incomes below a fixed figure to fall year on year. This has usually been the case since 1996/97. 'Relative' low income figures can be a better way of assessing whether Government policies are directing resources to those at the bottom of the income distribution, rather than if their incomes are simply rising with inflation.

There are good reasons to use both types of low-income measure, but it is important to be aware of the advantages and disadvantages associated with each. Something that neither measure is able to do is to tell us anything about the standard of living that anyone living below the threshold experiences.

Receipt of welfare benefits

In addition to measuring the number of people living on low incomes through the HBAI data, we can also use receipt of key welfare benefits to track the numbers of people living on low incomes. The key benefits usually referred to are jobseeker's allowance (JSA), incapacity benefit (IB), severe disablement allowance (SDA), disability living allowance (DLA), pension credit, income support (IS), and, from April 2004, child tax credit and child benefit.

IS is a means-tested benefit for people whose income falls below a specified level, or who have no other source of income. This may be because they are unable to work because they are sick, disabled, pregnant or caring for others. Income-based JSA replaced IS for unemployed people in 1996. It is a means-tested benefit paid to people registered as available for and actively seeking work, whose incomes fall below a specified level.

For claims which began prior to April 2004, IS and income-based JSA are made up of a personal allowance, an allowance for dependent children and premiums. The level of personal allowance varies according to partnership status (single, couple or lone parent) and age (varying for example between 16–17, 18–24 and over 25). Premiums are given for families, disabled children, carers and disabled adults. As for HBAI data,

IS levels vary according to family household type. With the introduction of child tax credit, allowances and premiums for dependent children have been replaced with child tax credit and child benefit. Since October 2005, pension credit has replaced IS for people aged 60 and over.

Table 2.3 shows the level of IS, or IS with child tax credit and child benefit, or pension credit for selected family types. These benefit levels represent a crude official indication of the minimum income required for living in Britain today.

How many people live in poverty in Scotland?

The previous section defined the three main ways in which poverty is measured in the UK. In this section, these definitions are used to estimate the number of people living in poverty in Scotland. Here, the focus is on the total number of people living in poverty. Estimates of the number of people living in poverty from sub-groups of the population (for example, by family type, or by local authority area) are considered in Chapter 4.

Child poverty

There was a steady growth in child poverty in Scotland and the UK over the last few decades of the twentieth century. By the turn of the century, it was well established that children were over-represented at the bottom of the income distribution and under-represented at the top: according to the annual HBAI report at this time, 'Children are now the group most likely to be in low-income households, and most likely to remain in low-income households for a long period of time'.[15]

The UK government and Scottish Executive's commitment to reduce child poverty is now beginning to arrest this trend. Table 2.4 reports the number of children in Scotland who are living in poverty and Figure 2.1 charts changes to the proportion of children living in poverty of all children in Scotland from 1994/95.

According to these Scottish Executive figures, 240,000 children living in Scotland are part of households whose income is so much lower than the typical income for households in Scotland that we can consider them to be living in poverty (60 per cent below median equivalised income). On the

Table 2.3:

Poverty lines as defined by means-tested benefits, tax credit and child benefit levels, Great Britain, April 2006

Family household type	Level
	£ per week
Single with no children, aged 16–17	34.60
Single with no children, aged 18–24	45.50
Single with no children, aged over 25	57.45
Couple, at least one aged 18 or over, with no children	90.10
Single, aged 16–17 with two children (aged 1 or over)	142.01
Single, aged 18 or over with two children (aged 1 or over)	164.86
Couple, both aged over 18 with two children (aged 1 or over)	197.51
Single pensioner	114.05
Couple pensioner	174.05

Sources: Department for Work and Pensions, *Income Support Statistics*, http://www.jobcentreplus.gov.uk/ JCP/Customers/WorkingAgeBenefits/IncomeSupport/index.html accessed 27 April 2006; Department for Work and Pensions, *The Pension Service*, http://www.thepensionservice.gov.uk/home.asp accessed 27 April 2006

other hand, 130,000 children in Scotland are living in households which have not experienced a real rise in income levels since 1998/99. In terms of proportions, and using the same Scottish Executive figures, nearly one in four children in Scotland (23 per cent) live in relative poverty and almost one in eight children in Scotland (13 per cent) live in absolute poverty.

As the figures above show, child poverty is at a disturbingly high level in Scotland. However, since 1996/97, the trend has been clearly and consistently toward the reduction of child poverty, falling from a high of 370,000 (33 per cent) of children living in absolute poverty to 130,000 (13 per cent) and from 370,000 (33 per cent) living in relative poverty to 240,000 (23 per cent) today.

Figure 2.2 compares the percentage of children living in households with incomes of below 60 per cent median earnings in Great Britain, to those from other government office regions and national regions in Great Britain for 2004/05.

There are discrepancies between the data provided in Figure 2.1 and Figure 2.2, which result from the use of a three-year rolled average for GB nations and regions (Figure 2.2), whereas Figure 2.1 uses single year totals alone. However, what is clear from Figure 2.2 is that fewer children

Table 2.4:

Number of children living in absolute poverty and relative poverty, Scotland, 1994/95 to 2004/05

Thousands

	94/95	95/96	96/97	97/87	98/99	99/00	00/01	01/02	02/03	03/04	04/05
Absolute poverty	340	370	370	330	310	280	220	170	170	160	130
Relative poverty	300	350	370	330	320	330	310	320	280	260	240

Source: Scottish Executive, *Scottish Households Below Average Income, 2004/05*, 2006, Tables 1 and 2

Note: Figures are derived from the *Family Resources Survey*. The McClements equivalisation scale has been used in the calculations and the figures refer to income after housing costs. Refer to Table 2.1 for definitions of absolute poverty (low income) and relative poverty (low income).

live in poverty in Scotland than in Wales and most regions in England. Indeed, only in the East and South East regions of England is there a lower level of child poverty.

Comparative data cast Scotland in a positive light, although this should not obscure the fact that many thousands of children in Scotland are currently living in poverty.

Households Below Average Income

Although children are the primary focus of the UK Government and Scottish Executive's anti-poverty activity, a fuller understanding of poverty in the UK requires a more broadly based analysis of poverty among the population as a whole.

Mirroring the presentation of evidence for child poverty, Table 2.5 reports the number of individuals in Scotland who are living in poverty and Figure 2.3 charts changes to the proportion of individuals living in poverty in Scotland from 1994/95.

According to these figures, 550,000 individuals are in households regarded as experiencing 'absolute poverty' (60 per cent below median equivalised household income at 1996/97 levels). 910,000 individuals in Scotland are living in households regarded as experiencing 'relative poverty' (60 per cent below median equivalised household income at current levels). In terms of proportions almost one in five individuals in Scotland

Figure 2.1:

Proportion of children living in absolute poverty and relative poverty, Scotland, 1994/95 to 2004/05

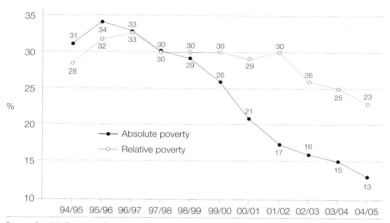

Source: Scottish Executive, *Scottish Households Below Average Income, 2004/05*, 2006, Tables 1 and 2

Note: Figures are derived from the *Family Resources Survey*. The McClements equivalisation scale has been used in the calculations and the figures refer to income after housing costs. Refer to Table 2.1 for definitions of absolute poverty (low income) and relative poverty (low income).

(18 per cent) live in relative poverty and more than one in ten individuals in Scotland (11 per cent) live in absolute poverty.

These figures show that it is not only child poverty that is a problem in Scotland. However, as with trends relating to child poverty, it should be acknowledged that since the mid-1990s, the trend has been clearly and consistently toward the reduction of poverty in Scotland, falling from a high of 1,230,000 (25 per cent) of people living in absolute poverty to 550,000 (11 per cent) and from 1,230,000 (25 per cent) living in relative poverty to 850,000 (18 per cent) today. Indeed, these latest figures suggest that following a decade of fluctuations around the one million mark, the number of individuals living in relative poverty in Scotland is now firmly below one million people.

Figure 2.4 compares the percentage of individuals in Scotland living in households with incomes of below 60 per cent median earnings for Great Britain, with those from other government office regions and national regions in Great Britain for 2004/05.

Figure 2.2:

Children living in low-income households in Scotland, and other parts of Great Britain, 2004/05 (low household income defined as below 60 per cent GB median income, after housing costs and including self-employed)

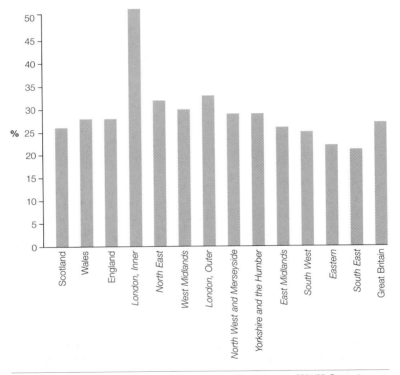

Source: Department for Work and Pensions, *Households Below Average Income, 2004/05*, Corporate Document Services, 2006, Table 4.9

Note: The differences for children in Scotland for 2004/05 can be accounted for in the difference in the use of a three-year rolled average for GB nations and regions in Figure 2.2, whereas Figure 2.1 and Table 2.4 use single year totals alone.

Notwithstanding the same data discrepancies between Figure 2.4 and Figure 2.3, which were highlighted for Figures 2.1 and 2.2, once again there is evidence to suggest that the level of poverty in Scotland compares favourably with that in other parts of Great Britain. The level of poverty in Scotland is marginally lower than that in Wales and most regions in

Figure 2.3:

Individuals with below 60 per cent GB median income, after housing costs and including self-employed, Scotland, 1994/95 to 2004/05

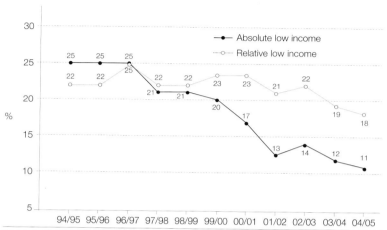

Source: Scottish Executive, *Scottish Households Below Average Income, 2004/05*, 2006, Tables 1 and 2

Note: Figures are derived from the *Family Resources Survey*. The McClements equivalisation scales have been used in the calculations and the figures refer to income after housing costs. Absolute low income is based on median income in 1996/97 (adjusted for inflation).

Table 2.5:

Individuals with below 60 per cent GB median income, after housing costs and including self-employed, Scotland, 1994/95 to 2004/05

Thousands

	94/95	95/96	96/97	97/98	98/99	99/00	00/01	01/02	02/03	03/04	04/05
Absolute low income	1,240	1,230	1,230	1,070	1,030	980	850	650	690	600	550
Relative low income	1,080	1,120	1,230	1,090	1,110	1,150	1,140	1,060	1,070	960	910

Source: Scottish Executive, *Scottish Households Below Average Income, 2004/05*, 2006, Tables 1 and 2

Note: Figures are derived from the *Family Resources Survey*. The McClements equivalisation scales have been used in the calculations and the figures refer to income after housing costs. Absolute low income is based on median income in 1996/97 (adjusted for inflation).

England. Indeed, only in the East, South East and South West regions of England is there a lower level of poverty. It is worth noting also that the significant proportion of individuals living in poverty in Inner London (well above the Scottish and Great Britain averages) will have an impact on the overall Great Britain average.

Once again though, although comparative data cast Scotland in a positive light, this should not be allowed to obscure the fact that many thousands of people in Scotland are currently living in poverty – more than half a million people if the more stringent measure of absolute poverty is used and just less than one million if we adopt the relative measure of poverty.

Receipt of welfare benefits

The contribution of welfare payments to income levels

The contribution of welfare payments to overall income (as opposed to wages, self-employment income, investments, tax credits and private pensions) can be used as an overall measure of the level of poverty. Table 2.6 summarises the components of weekly income in Scotland, and compares Scotland with other parts of the UK.

Welfare payments are an important source of household income in Scotland, although they are much less important than wages. Significantly, state pensions contribute an amount comparable to private pensions, and welfare payments (disability and general combined) contribute more than income generated through self-employment. Almost one-sixth of household income in Scotland comprises welfare payments and state pensions combined (Table 2.6). Scotland has a lower than average income sourced through self-employment. Average household income in Scotland is more reliant on welfare payments than in most regions in England, although less reliant than in Wales, Northern Ireland and the North West, North East and Yorkshire regions in England (Table 2.6).

This national overview informs our understanding of low income in that it specifies the contribution of welfare to overall income. However, the national picture on overall income may be obscured by high wages (of the few) – a better understanding of the incidence of poverty is gained when the number of recipients of welfare payments is considered.

Income support recipients

Table 2.7 shows the numbers of IS recipients in Scotland and the proportion of IS recipients among the whole population. Table 2.7 recognises

Figure 2.4:

Individuals living on a low income in Scotland, and other parts of Great Britain, 2004/05 (low household income defined as below 60 per cent GB median income, after housing costs and including self-employed)

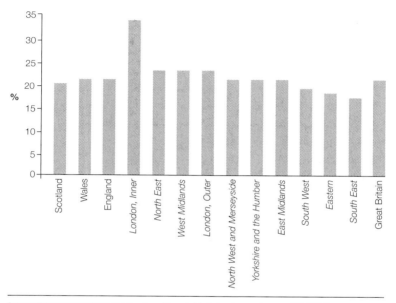

Source: Department for Work and Pensions, *Households Below Average Income, 2004/05*, Corporate Document Services, 2006, Table 3.6

Note: The differences for children in Scotland for 2004/05 can be accounted for in the use of a three-year rolled average for GB national regions in Figure 2.4, whereas Figure 2.3 and Table 2.5 use the 2004/05 year total alone.

that it is important to determine the number of partners and dependants of claimants in order to give a better estimate of the numbers living in poverty. It should be noted that dependency ratios vary for different client groups. Lone parents are more likely to have more dependants than pensioners, for example.

The total number of people in Scotland living on IS in February 2005 was 416,000. This includes claimants, their partners and dependants; 162,000 people were dependants of IS claimants. Collectively, these ben-

Table 2.6:
Components of weekly household income in Scotland, and other parts of the United Kingdom, 2004/05

	Wages/ salaries	Self- employment	Investments	Tax credits	Pension, state	Pension, other	Welfare, disability	Welfare, other	Other
	%	%	%	%	%	%	%	%	%
Scotland	65	6	2	1	7	7	3	6	2
Wales	58	10	2	2	8	8	4	6	2
Northern Ireland	60	12	1	2	6	5	4	7	2
England	65	9	2	1	6	7	2	5	2
London	71	10	2	1	4	4	1	5	3
North East	62	6	2	2	8	8	4	7	2
West Midlands	65	7	2	2	7	6	3	6	2
North West and Merseyside	63	7	2	2	7	7	3	7	2
Yorkshire and the Humber	64	6	2	2	7	8	3	7	2
East Midlands	66	8	2	1	7	7	2	5	2
South West	61	9	3	2	7	10	2	4	2
Eastern	65	11	2	1	6	8	2	4	2
South East	66	10	3	1	5	8	1	3	2
United Kingdom	65	9	2	1	6	7	2	5	2

Source: M Chung and others, *Family Resources Survey, 2004/05*, Department for Work and Pensions, 2006, Table 3.1

eficiaries of IS make up just over 8 per cent of the population living in Scotland.

The percentage of the Scottish population receiving IS (8.2 per cent) was above the Great Britain average of 7.6 per cent. Higher proportions of the population in Scotland receive IS than in six of the nine regions in England.

IS is the welfare payment measure that is most commonly used to estimate the number of people living in poverty. However, it could be argued that a more broadly based analysis of welfare payments would provide a fuller understanding of the proportion of people living in poverty, or at least on a low income, in Scotland.

Table 2.7:

Income support recipients in Scotland, and other parts of Great Britain, February 2005

	Type of beneficiary				
	All	**Claimants**	**Partner**	**Dependant**	**% of whole population**
	000s	000s	000s	000s	000s
Scotland	416	229	25	162	8.2
Wales	261	126	20	114	8.9
England	3,736	1,782	235	1,720	7.5
London	801	367	36	397	10.8
North East	239	118	19	103	9.4
North West	635	314	43	278	9.3
West Midlands	428	196	29	203	8.0
Yorkshire and the Humber	388	186	29	173	7.8
East Midlands	269	128	19	122	6.3
Eastern	303	144	18	141	5.5
South West	272	137	18	117	5.4
South East	399	191	22	186	4.9
Great Britain	4,413	2,137	281	1,996	7.6

Source: Department for Work and Pensions, *Income Support Statistical Enquiry February 2005*, 2006, Table 4.3

Note: Income support beneficiary figures were affected by the new tax credits introduced in April 2003 and the transfer of claimants over 60 to pension credit in October 2003.

Range of welfare payments

Table 2.8 shows the proportion of households in receipt of different types of benefit and summary counts of the proportion of households in receipt of benefits, income-related benefits, tax credits and state support. Data is presented for all national regions in the UK.

For the most part, only small differences are evident between Scotland and other national regions in the UK for specific benefit types. However, it is notable that households in Scotland are most likely to receive housing benefit (HB) and council tax benefit (CTB) – for example, 14 per cent, compared with 11 per cent in England for HB, and 19 per cent, compared with 15 per cent in England for CTB. Both of these benefits are means tested and are administered by the local author-ity. HB can be claimed by anyone who is liable to pay rent and whose income falls below a prescribed level, and is, therefore, available both to people receiving social security benefits and to those who are in employment. The higher levels of HB receipt in Scotland may be a consequence of the high proportion of people in public sector housing.[16] CTB can be claimed by anyone who is liable to pay council tax on the accommodation which is normally their home and who has sufficiently low income.

However, the net effect of all these benefit receipts is that almost one in every four households in Scotland receive an income-related benefit (23 per cent). This is markedly higher than the UK average of 19 per cent and higher than the levels reported for each of the other national regions. Although levels of receipt of non-income-related benefits are significantly lower in Scotland, the most relevant data for examining poverty is the benefits that are income-based.

On this wider review of receipt of income-based benefits, levels of poverty in Scotland are substantially significant (23 per cent of households) and poverty is more widespread in Scotland than in other national regions of the UK.

Key benefits

An analysis of the receipt of key benefits – JSA, IB, SDA, DLA and IS – sits between the narrow focus on IS payments alone and the broader overview of receipt of all welfare payments. Table 2.9 reports the receipt of key benefits in Scotland, disaggregates this by gender and compares Scotland with other parts of Great Britain.

Over half a million people living in Scotland claimed a key benefit in May 2004, equalling almost one in six people in Scotland (Table 2.9). Claimant rates were slightly higher for men (17.9 per cent, compared with 16.2 per cent for women). Claimant rates in Scotland were significantly above the average for Great Britain (13.6 per cent) and were only lower than claimant rates in Wales (18.4 per cent), the North West of England (17.3 per cent) and the North East of England (18.9 per cent).

This data confirms the finding from the more broadly based review of welfare payment receipt, that poverty is more widespread in Scotland than in most other parts of Great Britain.

Conclusion

This chapter has set out some of the key issues related to the measurement and definition of poverty in Scotland. We have also alluded to

Table 2.8:
Households receiving different types of benefits by national region in the UK, 2004/05

	Scotland	England	Wales	Northern Ireland	UK
	%	%	%	%	%
Working tax credit	4	4	5	4	4
Child tax credit	13	13	14	15	13
Income support	7	6	7	8	6
Pension credit	7	6	7	5	6
Housing benefit	14	11	11	13	11
Council tax benefit	19	15	16	2	15
Retirement pension	25	25	27	22	25
Widows' benefits	1	1	1	1	1
Jobseeker's allowance	2	2	2	3	2
Incapacity benefit	5	4	7	7	5
Severe disablement allowance	–	–	–	1	–
Attendance allowance	3	3	5	5	3
Carer's allowance	1	1	2	3	1
Disability living allowance (care component)	6	5	8	11	5
Disability living allowance (mobility component)	7	5	9	10	5
Industrial injuries disablement benefit	1	1	1	1	1
War disablement or war widow's pension	1	1	1	–	1
Child benefit	22	23	23	27	23
Any income-related benefit	23	19	20	21	19
Any non-income-related benefit	56	56	61	59	56
All in receipt of benefit	60	58	64	62	59
All in receipt of tax credits	14	13	15	15	14
All not in receipt of state support	40	41	35	37	41
Sample size	5,312	24,051	1,462	2,377	33,202

Source: M Chung and others, *Family Resources Survey, 2004/05*, Department for Work and Pensions, 2006, Table 3.14

Table 2.9:
Claimants of key benefits by sex in Scotland, and other parts of Great Britain, May 2004

	All		Men		Women	
	000s	%	000s	%	000s	%
Scotland	538	17.1	289	17.9	249	16.2
Wales	322	18.4	169	18.9	153	18.0
England	3,985	13.0	2,063	13.0	1,922	13.0
North East	292	18.9	157	19.8	135	18.1
North West	712	17.3	377	17.8	335	16.8
West Midlands	464	14.4	243	14.4	222	14.3
Yorkshire and the Humber	439	14.4	236	15.0	203	13.8
London	694	14.2	341	13.5	352	14.9
East Midlands	319	12.3	166	12.3	153	12.3
South West	311	10.5	164	10.6	148	10.4
Eastern	325	9.8	162	9.4	163	10.3
South East	430	8.7	218	8.5	212	8.9
Great Britain	4,845	13.6	2,521	13.7	2,325	13.6

Source: Department for Work and Pensions, *Work and Pensions Statistics 2004*, 2005, Table 24

Note: Key benefits are jobseeker's allowance, incapacity benefit, severe disability allowance, disability living allowance and income support.

Denominator for percentages is all adults/males/females of working age.

some of the related, and complex, issues surrounding the relationship between poverty and social exclusion, social inclusion and social justice. Our discussions so far suggest that low income is central to any definition of poverty, whether relative or absolute. The concepts of inclusion and exclusion broaden the understanding of poverty and better represent the multi-dimensional nature of poverty. Such concepts also help to remind us of the consequences and experience of living in poverty, an issue that will be covered in more depth in Chapter 5. For it is also important to remember that the fundamental concern is '... the relationship between low income and a person's ability to live the kind of life she or he values... income is a means to an end rather than an end in itself'.[17]

The figures in this chapter have outlined the broad trends in low incomes using three different measures. All this data shows that income poverty is a significant problem in Scotland, despite some real improvements in recent years. We have highlighted the decline in child poverty, down by a quarter since 1996/97, and the more modest fall in poverty for all individuals. These declines should be welcomed and those responsible for the fall should be encouraged to do more. However, as will be shown in Chapter 4, not all groups in our society have felt the benefit of these falls and more will need to be done to ensure that all those affected by poverty in Scotland feel the benefits of anti-poverty policy.

Notes

1 R Lister, *Poverty*, Polity Press, 2004

2 P Townsend, *Poverty in the United Kingdom*, Penguin, 1979

3 C Oppenheim and L Harker, *Poverty: the facts*, Child Poverty Action Group, 1996

4 Department for Work and Pensions, *Reaching Out: the UK national action plan on social inclusion 2006-08*, DWP, 2006, available online at: http://www.socia linclusion.org.uk/publications/reachingoutfull.pdf

5 J Roll, *Understanding Poverty: a guide to the concepts and measures*, Family Policy Studies Centre, 1992

6 D Miller, 'What is Social Justice?', in N Pearce and W Paxton (eds), *Social Justice: building a fairer Britain*, Politicos, 2005

7 The Commission on Social Justice, *The Justice Gap*, Institute for Public Policy Research,1993

8 Department for Work and Pensions, *Measuring Child Poverty*, DWP, 2003, available online at: http://www.dwp.gov.uk/ofa/related/final_conclusions.pdf

9 Department for Work and Pensions, *Opportunity for All: eighth annual report*, The Stationery Office, 2006, available online at: http://www.dwp.gov.uk/ofa/reports/latest.asp

10 See note 3

11 Eurostat Task Force, 'Recommendations on Social Exclusion and Poverty Statistics', paper presented to the 26-27 November meeting of the EU Statistical Programme Committee, 1998

12 A Sinfield, *Tackling and Preventing Poverty*, Memorandum to Scottish Affairs Committee, March 2000

13 Scottish Executive, *Households Below Average Income 2004/05*, 2006, available at: http://www.scotland.gov.uk/Publications/2006/03/08155404/1

14 See note 8

15 Department for Work and Pensions, *Households Below Average Income 2000/01*, Corporate Document Services, 2001, available online at: http://www.dwp.gov.uk/asd/hbai.asp

16 National Statistics, 'Housing', *Regional Trends* 39, 2006, Table 6.3, p114, available online at: http://www.statistics.gov.uk/downloads/theme_compendia/Regional_Trends_39/RT39_Housing.pdf

17 See note 1

Three

Factors leading to poverty

John H McKendrick and
John Dickie

This chapter accounts for the causes of poverty in Scotland. This is by no means a straightforward task, as the factors which create and keep people in poverty cannot be reduced to a single cause, which directly and exclusively results in poverty. By way of introduction, we outline four complications, which are encountered when we seek to explain why poverty exists.

First, there are several possible reasons why people experience poverty. This chapter is structured into four sections, each of which considers one of the four broad causes of poverty. Poverty is sometimes attributed to the **behaviour of individuals**. Here, we will consider how personal knowledge of the 'feckless poor', grounded in everyday social theorising based on stereotypes, is used to support the viewpoint that poverty results from the failings of individuals. We argue that this type of explanation is of limited value in accounting for poverty in Scotland. Poverty can be attributed to **social factors**, that is, characteristics which define groups of people and which place additional demands on their resources and/or make them more vulnerable to other poverty-inducing factors. Here, we consider the social factors which induce poverty among the groups we identify as being vulnerable to poverty in Chapter 4. Poverty in Scotland can also be attributed to **political factors**, that is, the extent to which government is prepared to intervene to tackle poverty and the effectiveness of these interventions. Here, we focus on the significance of the UK Parliament and the Scottish Executive, considering factors such as the national minimum wage, benefits, New Deal, taxation, area regeneration and employability strategies. Finally, poverty can also be attributed to **economic factors**, for example, the strength of the macro-economy and the distribution of income across the population.

Second, the poverty experienced by individuals tends to result from more than one of these poverty-inducing factors. For example, the susceptibility to poverty of single adults without children living in remote rural

be attributed to the high per unit head costs of maintain-
that is, no economies of scale to be gained through living
social factor), limited opportunity in the local labour market
nt living wage (economic factor), and a lack of state inter-
l poverty is deemed a less pressing priority for policy inter-
al factor). Progress in some factors may not be sufficient to
counter... her persistent poverty-inducing circumstances.

Third, the factors which cause people to be poor are inter-related.
For example, the susceptibility to poverty of lone parents might be attributed to restricted labour market options, given lone parents' need to com-
bine work with parental responsibilities (social factor), resulting in difficulties
in accessing employment which pays a decent living wage (economic factor). Here, the social situation influences the economic possibilities, both of
which contribute to the poverty experienced by the individual.

Finally, the ways in which poverty-inducing factors influence individuals can be complex, hidden and indirect. For example, Scotland has a
small domestic market and it is very dependent on exports and inward
investment. It is, therefore, vulnerable to changes in global and UK national economic trends. However, the extent to which these macro-economic forces result in poverty is dependent on a host of intervening factors
such as the economic strategy of transnational corporations, induce-
ments and support from inward investment agencies, and the ability of the
local economy to absorb job losses.

Individual factors

Many of us have anecdotal knowledge of individuals who seem to do little to arrest the poverty which they experience, or of individuals who would
be classified as 'poor' using official data sources, but who supplement
their income through the informal economy. Then again, many may not
understand why people can be poor given state support through social
security (for example, income support), safeguards against low income
(for example, national minimum wage) and the array of opportunities provided in communities and by the state to enable people to lift themselves
out of poverty (for example, New Deal programmes), or to reduce the
costs of living on a low income (for example, local food co-operatives).
Furthermore, public debate on poverty in Scotland often draws on deeply
entrenched stereotypes, often rationalising people's life trajectory on the

basis of where they live or their social profile (for example, 'she's poor because she's a 'single mother' from Ferguslie Park'). In short, individuals are deemed to be the primary cause of their poverty and official measures of poverty are perceived to overstate the problem. Such arguments carry some intuitive appeal.

There are five key points which critique the line of thinking that attributes poverty to the action or inaction of individuals. First, poverty experienced by children has little to do with children's own actions; the 240,000 children experiencing poverty in Scotland (Table 2.4), do so exclusively on account of chance, that is, the fortune or accident of birth, which determines the families into which they are born – not all of the poor can be held responsible for the poverty they experience. Second, reducing poverty to the actions of individuals does not allow the possibility of poverty being influenced by other factors, and takes no account of the large-scale structural (social, political and economic) forces that shape people's lives. As was argued in the introduction, the causes of poverty are multi-faceted. Third, on closer analysis, what appear to be 'individual-level' factors, are often social factors. For example, the understanding that poverty is transmitted down through generations of the same family is often perceived to be a problem of the individual, when more correctly it should be viewed as a social factor, that is, the cultural influence of family and community life. And as James McCormick of the Scottish Council Foundation argued so persuasively many years ago in an earlier CPAG publication, poor places keep people poor.[1] Fourth, focusing on individual behaviour as a cause of poverty risks distracting attention from the social, economic and political causes of poverty over which it is possible for policy makers to exert influence and which, therefore, hold most potential for successful policy intervention. Finally, there is a numerical challenge to those who argue that poverty is the fault of individuals. According to Scottish Executive estimates, 910,000 people experience poverty in Scotland (Table 2.5). There can be no credibility in the argument that almost one-fifth of the population in Scotland experience poverty on account of their own personal failings.

Social factors

As the following chapter demonstrates, the distribution of poverty in Scotland is uneven across social groups and places. This must not, however, lead to an explanation for Scotland's poverty that is based on describing the changing composition of Scotland's population. Thus, for example, the changing composition of families in Scotland since the early 1970s – including the rise in lone parenthood – should not, *per se*, be used to explain the corresponding growth in poverty at that time. It is more accurate to explain that the rise of poverty was down to the high risk of poverty faced by a group growing in size and the failure of policies to intervene to reduce this risk. There is clearly an association between these trends (and between the extent of poverty and other social trends), but we gain no insight into the root causes of poverty. Most problematically, this approach encourages scapegoating and a culture of blame (for example, lone parenthood causes poverty).

However, there are common shared characteristics among social groups that make them more susceptible to poverty and make the escape route from poverty more difficult than otherwise would be the case. Table 3.1 summarises some of the social factors which are experienced by the groups identified in the following chapter as being particularly susceptible to poverty.

Of course, Table 3.1 is only a summary overview of some of the main social factors which may cause or exacerbate the poverty experienced by groups of people in Scotland. Although space does not permit presentation of evidence which would justify the assertions made in Table 3.1, further comment is provided for two of the group-specific poverty-inducing factors. First, identifying the national minimum wage as a contributory factor for young people's poverty seems counter-intuitive. Second, the existence of gender pay gaps is at odds with long-standing government legislation and recent steps to promote equal pay among local authorities in Scotland through single status pay agreements.

The introduction of the national minimum wage – one of the four factors listed as poverty-inducing for young people – has improved pay rates for younger people. Of particular note, is the introduction of a national minimum wage for workers aged between 16 and 17 years old in 2004. However, on closer analysis, it could be argued that the national minimum wage could be a more effective aid in tackling poverty among young people. It justifies relatively lower wages for young people; the main rate for workers aged 22 and over increased to £5.35 an hour on 1 October 2006, which is higher than the 'development' rates set for young adults between 18 and 21 years (£4.45 an hour) and 16–17-year-olds (£3.30 an hour). Thus, while the national minimum wage has tackled some of the worst pay excesses, low pay among young people remains

Table 3.1:
Social factors as a cause of poverty

Group	Factors (examples)
Lifecycle	
Children	Limited ability to earn money to lift themselves out of poverty.
	Poverty status is dependent on their parents or guardians.
Youth	Lower wages for this age group, with lower rate of the national minimum wage.
	Benefit rates are lower for this age group.
	Lack of opportunity to accumulate wealth which could be used to ameliorate the effects of short-term bouts of poverty.
	Poverty may be a transitional state associated with periods of education and training – for example, through New Deal schemes.
Working-age adults	Welfare system is oriented toward providing for young and old.
Pensioners	Many have not provided for private pensions, having been brought up believing that the state pension would provide for their needs in old age. Thus, pensioner poverty reflects the circumstances of their working lives. If they were unemployed for long periods, worked in low-paid jobs, had insecure or interrupted work histories, were ill for long periods, or involved in unpaid work, they are more likely to be poor.
	State pension complexity results in low take-up.
	Higher heating and fuel costs.
Families and households	
Lone parents	Cost of childcare.
	Availability of childcare (barrier to participation in the labour market).
	Work-life balance (for example, mismatch between school hours and working hours).
Partnered parents	Unequal distribution of income among householders.
	Unequal expenditure responsibilities among householders (for example, women spending on all family members).
Childless adults	Welfare system is oriented toward providing for young, old and families with children.
	Inadequate income support rates for single adults.
Social	
Work status	Low pay.
	Costs associated with a 'flexible' workforce.
	Under-employment.
Gender	Costs associated with being primary carers of children (interrupted work histories and having to work in lower paid jobs).
	Gender segregation in the labour market (over-concentration in lower paid jobs).

Gender gap in pay.

Intra-household distribution of income.

Ethnicity	Pensioner poverty among immigrants (having not built up pension entitlement on account of being engaged in low-paid work and beginning to contribute in the middle of their working lives).
	Language barriers during transitional phase for immigrants.
	Racist harassment and victimisation; stereotyping.
	Tendency to work in sectors of the economy in which wages are low (especially those of Pakistani and Bangladeshi backgrounds).
Disability/illness	Extra costs associated with managing particular disability or illness, such as medicine, housing adaption or transport costs (the majority of disabled people do not receive additional costs).
	Higher cost of living associated with shopping locally (difficulty in accessing more distant, but cheaper, supermarkets).
	Costs of caring.
	Discrimination based on stereotyping.
	Disabling environments, hampering access.

Place

Local authorities	(Under)strength of local economy.
Rural areas	Lack of public transport in rural areas (restricting access).
	Additional cost of transport in rural areas (for example, necessity of running a car).
	Fewer public services
	Low pay.
	Higher cost of living.
	More restricted employment/career opportunities.
Local area	By definition, these will vary across place.

a major problem among young adults and it gives credibility to lower rates of pay for younger workers.

The right of women to equal pay has been enshrined in UK legislation since the Equal Pay Act in 1975 and has since been strengthened by amendments, such as that in 1984 to ensure equal pay for equivalent work. More recently, in 1999 single status agreements were reached between the trade unions and local government in Scotland to ensure verifiable pay equality between men and woman. However, by 2006, these agreements had not been implemented and the unions are concerned that single status is being implemented by imposing pay cuts and by driving down wages through job evaluation.[2] The employment status of women in Scotland is similar to that which applies in the rest of the UK; fewer women are economically active (76 per cent, compared

Table 3.2:

Gender gap in median gross weekly earnings of full-time employees by occupational group, Scotland, April 2004

	Gross median weekly earnings		
	Men £	Women £	Women as a % of men
Managers and senior officials	614.20	479.60	0.78
Professional occupations	617.70	551.00	0.89
Associated professional and technical	500.40	442.40	0.88
Administrative and secretarial	332.30	291.80	0.88
Skilled trade	386.50	265.60*	0.69
Personal service	307.40	269.00	0.88
Sales and customer service	250.60*	230.70	0.92
Process, plant and machine operatives	353.40	261.90*	0.74
Elementary	300.00	219.00	0.73
All occupations	432.20	345.50	0.80

Source: Scottish Executive, *Scottish Economic Statistics 2005*, Scottish Executive, 2005, Table 4.16 (sourced from Annual Survey of Hours and Earnings 2004)

Note: Full-time employees on adult rates whose pay was not affected by absence for the survey period.

* low sample size and result should be treated with caution.

with 83 per cent of men in 2005),[3] the concentration across industry sector is highly gendered (71.5 per cent of workers in public administration, education and health are women, compared with 18 per cent in energy, water and supply[4]), and while equivalent numbers of men and women are employed (1,095,000 men and 1,084,000 women in Scotland in 2005), men are almost three times as likely to be self-employed, twice as likely to be working full time, while women are more than three times as likely to be employed part time.[5] While these gender patterns in work would explain why men earn more than women, what is particularly disconcerting is that the pay gap between men and women is evident across all occupation types – when like is compared with like. Table 3.2 shows how women's median weekly earnings in Scotland compare to men's across occupational types, ranging from as low as 69 per cent of male earnings in skilled trades up to a 92 per cent in sales and customer services. Across occupations, women on average earn only 80 per cent of their male counterparts. Indeed, since these figures include only full-time employees, excluding the often poorly paid part-time workforce, these are likely to underestimate true gender inequality in pay.

However, the gendered character of poverty should not be accepted as inevitable in the world in which we live. For example, implementation of single status should make inroads to reduce the gender pay gap in Scotland, as should the UK-wide gender equality duty from April 2007. Indeed, over the long term, and acknowledging that personal pension provision will be increasingly important for future generations, it is notable that the gender gap in personal pension provision in Great Britain (whereby more men than women had personal pension provision) has now been reversed for those aged under 35 (Figure 3.1).

Political factors

Government action – or inaction – is one of the key factors which determines the extent and level of poverty in Scotland. To their credit, both the UK Government and the Scottish Executive have committed themselves to eradicate child poverty within a generation. However, poverty is also experienced in households without children and our governments have been less specific on setting targets to eradicate poverty for people within these households. Furthermore, the effectiveness of the strategies used by them to tackle child poverty must also be considered. Given their commitment, the correct questions to answer are, 'are our governments doing enough?' and 'how effective are our government interventions?' Here, we summarise the array of anti-poverty interventions introduced by the UK Parliament and the Scottish Executive in recent years.

Opportunity for All and *Closing the Opportunity Gap*

As was discussed in Chapter 1, both the UK Government and the Scottish Executive have pursued overarching, multi-dimensional strategies to address the poverty and social exclusion experienced by the most vulnerable. *Opportunity for All*[6] is beyond the remit of concern for this edition of *Poverty in Scotland* and *Closing the Opportunity Gap* has only recently moved beyond the stage of planning and design to commissioning the first evaluation of the programme.[7] We acknowledge the significance of both these programmes, but instead focus only on those

Figure 3.1:

Without pension provision by age and sex, Great Britain, 2004/05

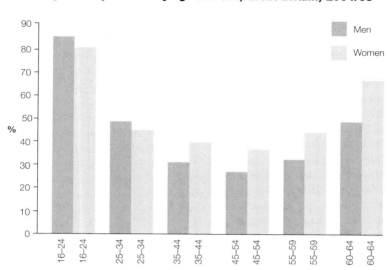

Source: Department for Work and Pensions, *Family Resources Survey, 2004/05*, 2005, Table 7.12

Note: Percentage of adults who are neither students nor retired with occupational, personal or stakeholder pension scheme.

aspects of governments' intervention, which have sought to influence the level of poverty currently experienced in Scotland.

UK Government

The UK Government retained responsibility following devolution for the main levers of control over poverty in Scotland – that is, the welfare system and taxation.

Benefits

Social security protects the vulnerable from the worst excesses of poverty. For example, in February 2005, it was estimated that 416,000 people in Scotland (one in every 12 people) benefited from income support alone.[8]

However, there are four limitations to the way in which the UK Parliament uses social security as a poverty-reduction strategy. First, the level of benefits has been tied to prices which, although ensuring that the spending power of welfare recipients is maintained year-on-year, also implies that the value of benefits has declined year-on-year as increases in prices have been lower than increases in average incomes. Relatively speaking, benefit recipients are becoming poorer compared with wage earners. Second, the UK Parliament subscribes to a welfare-to-work strategy through which it seeks to 'make work pay'. Although there is evidence that this approach has been successful in assisting people to escape poverty, this is an ineffective anti-poverty strategy for those who cannot work, for those for whom work is not available and for those who undertake unpaid work. Third, although UK Parliament policies are having some beneficial effect in reducing the level and intensity of child poverty – for example, the value of the universal child benefit has increased in real terms – the use of social security to tackle child poverty falls short of being a universal approach to overcome poverty, as social security is deployed in a more limited fashion to tackle the poverty of claimants without children. It might be more accurate to assert that the UK Parliament uses social security as a *child* poverty reduction strategy. Finally, the UK Parliament is not averse to using the social security system to effect behavioural change in a way that over-rides its poverty-reduction credentials. Thus, it sees fit to withdraw some benefits from those who do not comply with New Deal programmes. Although there are differences of opinion over the moral legitimacy of using such punitive measures, they clearly demonstrate that the poverty-reducing value of social security can be over-ridden by other goals.

It also worth considering at greater length some of the main ways in which social security offers more (or less) support to overcome the poverty of particular groups of people. Here, we consider young adults, childless adults, lone parents and pensioners.

Social security is less effective in overcoming poverty among young people. Young people under 25 are not eligible for the same rates of benefit as people aged 25 or over. Those aged 18–24 may only claim reduced rates of income support, while young people aged 16–17 have no automatic entitlement to benefit, and can claim only in very restricted circumstances. On the other hand, the New Deal for Young People was introduced in April 1998. It is compulsory for all 18–24-year-olds who have been unemployed for at least six months. It aims to help young unemployed people into jobs and increase their employability. By May 2006

80,520 young people in Scotland had gone into jobs from the New Deal, of which 67,940 (84 per cent) were sustained.[9]

Anti-poverty policy has neglected childless adults and as a result there has been no decline in the number of working-age adults without children living in poverty since 1997. Family Budget Unit research shows that income support rates for single adults are insufficient to provide even a 'low cost but acceptable' standard of living.[10] This also has shortcomings for addressing child poverty; poverty experienced by (childless) mothers-to-be and pregnant women has a damaging impact on childbirth, and infant health and mortality, undermining progress on reducing child poverty.[11]

The welfare-to-work approach has resulted in a significant increase in the proportion of lone parents in work, rising from 44 per cent in 1997, to 57 per cent in 2006.[12] Nevertheless, a substantial number of lone parents are without work. The UK Parliament's welfare reform Green Paper proposes extending compulsory work-focused interviews for lone parents at the same time as introducing a new premium for lone parents taking steps toward returning to work.[13] However, research tends to show that the main barriers to work for lone parents are the cost and availability of childcare, illness or disability of a child, lack of opportunities for work, and low levels of skill and confidence.[14] Lack of qualifications remains a barrier for many lone parents. Around one-half of lone parents on income support have no academic or technical qualifications, only one-fifth are qualified up to NVQ2 level, and only 3 per cent are qualified to degree level.[15] The mix of punitive and reward strategies proposed in the Green Paper may be ineffective, unless action is taken to address the underlying issues that influence lone parents' labour market participation.

Government recognition that affordable childcare is a major factor in poverty reduction for families, and its commitment to work-based solutions to family poverty, have led to a variety of policies and programmes to boost childcare as part of an anti-poverty strategy in Scotland and in the rest of the UK. Recent analysis for the Joseph Rowntree Foundation found that UK childcare policy has come a long way since 1998.[16] By 2005, 582,000 new childcare and early education places had been created by supporting a mixed economy of provision through complex supply-side and demand-led funding packages. However, the report concludes that the childcare element of working tax credit was 'not particularly successful; in 2005 only 223,800 lone parents claimed it out of 1.06 million who could have potentially done so (as they were in receipt of working tax credit). Also, the average amount paid to all parents was low, at £51 per week in April 2005.[17] Parents in the UK still paid the bulk of their childcare costs, 75 per cent compared with an average of 25–30 per cent in the Organisation for Economic Co-operation and Development nations.[18] The result is that work often does not pay, with estimates suggesting that 54 per cent of lone parents working a 30-hour week for the minimum wage would be worse off if their childcare costs were equivalent to the maximum amount available under the childcare subsidy (then £135/week for one child).'

State pensions and benefits make up half of the average pensioner household income, and so remains pensioners' most important single source of income. Older pensioners, women and those on low incomes are even more dependent on state support. Since 1997, significant extra state support has been provided to pensioners. However, much of this has been means-tested, creating a system widely viewed as too complex and which leaves many pensioners without the support to which they are entitled. £4 billion worth of means-tested benefits went unclaimed in 2003/04 with evidence that it is those excluded who miss out, including people with disabilities, from minority ethnic communities and those living in isolated rural areas.[19] Problems of take-up and system complexity have led to organisations campaigning on behalf of older people to call for increases in the basic state pension to a level adequate to cover basic food, fuel and travel needs. These organisations have broadly welcomed the recommendation of the 2005 Turner Report for a basic state pension and second state pension, linked to earnings and above the level of means-tested benefits.[20]

Taxation

Higher earners pay more tax than lower earners in absolute terms, although not, as we shall see, as high a proportion of their income. For example in 2004/05, the average annual amount paid by the richest fifth of households in the UK was £16,760 in direct taxation and £7,330 in indirect taxation; in contrast, the average amount paid by the poorest fifth of households in the UK was £1,030 in direct taxation and £2,860 in indirect taxation.[21]

It must be recognised that taxation, *per se*, does not lead to a reduction in income inequality or a reduction in poverty. Rather, taxation – direct and indirect – are elements of a broader government strategy through which cash benefits (welfare support) is added to original income (for example, wages and investments) to give **gross income** (stage one). Gross income is then subject to direct taxation to give **disposable**

income (stage two). In 'disposing of this income', we are liable to indirect taxation. At this point, two calculations can be made to help us understand the impact of government intervention on income. First, the sum of the indirect taxes can be deducted from the disposable income to give us a measure of **post-tax income** (stage three – that is, [original income + cash benefits] – [direct taxation + indirect taxation]). Finally, we can take account of the benefits in kind – for example, education, health, social services, to give us a measure of **final income**. Taxation is the means through which government can redistribute earnings through cash benefits and benefits in kind.

Two criticisms can be made against the effectiveness of taxation as a means to tackle income poverty. First, taxation reduces the incomes of those on already low incomes; the poorest fifth of households in the UK have £3,890 deducted in taxation from a gross income of £10,690 (36.4 per cent of gross income is deducted in taxation).[22] In fairness, it could be argued that, to some extent, this is an administrative necessity as it would otherwise be too complex to refrain from taxing low-income groups, particularly at the point of consumption for indirect taxes. Second, although higher earners pay more in absolute sums, the lowest earning fifth of households in the UK pay a greater share of their gross income in taxation – for example, the 'tax burden' on the lowest-earning fifth (36.4 per cent) is higher than the highest earning households (35.6 per cent of the gross income of the highest earning fifth of households is deducted in tax). Indirect taxes and the direct council tax are particularly regressive. For example, the poorest fifth pay three times the proportion of their gross income on council tax (5.1 per cent, compared with 1.7 per cent of the highest earning fifth) and twice the proportion of their income on indirect taxes (26.8 per cent, compared with 10.8 per cent). It should come as no surprise, as we will consider below, that there has been little change in income inequality in recent years.

Scottish Executive

Although not able to dictate who receives cash benefits, the Scottish Executive can influence the extent and level of poverty in Scotland through using its tax-varying powers, by wholesale area regeneration, by creating the conditions necessary to facilitate the labour market participation of those without work, and by intervening to provide benefits in kind.

Area regeneration

Scotland has a long history of organising wholesale regeneration of what are perceived to be problem places; from the regeneration of the Maryhill Corridor and the Glasgow Eastern Area Renewal schemes in the 1970s, through the Areas of Priority Treatment identified by Strathclyde Regional Council in the1980s, Social Inclusion Partnerships in the late 1990s, and now community planning partnerships (see Chapter 17), there have been a succession of attempts to regenerate places for the better.

Although the enduring presence of the same places in successive area regeneration schemes points to the limitations and difficulties of an area-based approach, there have been some high-profile successes, such as Dundee's central waterfront, Leith docks and Glasgow's Merchant City and Clydeside. *People and Place* brings together the Scottish Executive's current thinking on regeneration policy and describes a five-pronged approach to work in partnership, set geographic priorities, redevelop land and property, create mixed communities and foster vibrant communities.[23] Time will tell whether the Scottish Executive's current plans for regenerating place will be more successful than previous attempts to solve the inter-related problems of Scotland's most deprived communities.

Employability strategies

Although it is a term that is widely used, 'employability' can mean a variety of things in different contexts. In the Scottish Executive's recently published employability framework, *Workforce Plus*, it is defined as '... the combination of factors and processes which enable people to progress towards or get into employment, to stay in employment and to move on in the workplace.'[24] To improve employability is, therefore, to address the barriers that people face in returning to the labour market, both individual and institutional, and to ensure that they have the correct support to stay in the labour market. Given the wide range of barriers that people can encounter, the type of policy interventions potentially covered by employability strategies is very broad indeed.

The Scottish Executive recently published its *More Choices, More Chances*[25] action plan to reduce the proportion of young people not in education, employment or training (NEET) in Scotland, alongside the Workforce Plus framework. The plan aims to reduce the number of young people becoming NEET, ensure all agencies and programmes involved with young people, from schools and colleges to the careers service and enterprise agencies, take ownership of, and focus on preventing and developing routes out of NEET status. The numbers of young people NEET is to become a key indicator of the success of those services and programmes.

The Scottish Executive is also seeking to address the lack of good quality, affordable childcare, especially in deprived areas, through its childcare strategy and more specifically in relation to tackling poverty through the Working for Families fund, an evaluation of which is expected in 2007 (see Chapters 12 and 16).

Benefits in kind

Two devolved interventions of particular note are free personal and nursing care for the elderly and free national bus travel for older and disabled people. These are examples of the way in which the Scottish Executive has been able to provide benefits in kind to enhance the 'income' of groups with a disproportionate share of Scotland's poverty. According to the Scottish Executive, it has invested £553 million since July 2002 for the provision of free personal and nursing care for everyone in Scotland aged 65 and over who needs it, whether at home, in hospital or in a care home.[26] Scotland-wide free bus travel for older and disabled people started on 1 April 2006, allowing free travel on virtually all local registered services and long-distance bus services within Scotland available to the general public, without peak-time restrictions. The scheme is nationwide and is not restricted to within the boundaries of local authorities.[27] However, despite pressure, ministers have to date resisted taking a similar universal approach to providing free school meals.

Economic factors

Macro-economy

The performance of the macro-economy is one possible reason for the existence of poverty. The logic is that there will be an inverse relationship between the economy and the extent and level of poverty – that is, the stronger the economy, the lower the intensity and extent of poverty.

According to the Scottish Executive's most recent *Scottish Economic Report*,[28] the Scottish economy is strong and continues to grow. There is much evidence that can be cited to support this point. For example, in 2005, Scotland's GVA (Gross Value Added) continued its stable pattern of long-term growth; employment reached an all-time high and unemployment fell to its lowest rate on record; in early 2006, Scotland's employment rate was higher than that of the rest of Great Britain and, for the first time in ten years, Scotland's unemployment rate matched that of Great Britain.

Although total employment has risen faster in Scotland than in Great Britain as a whole in recent years (1998-),[29] this has been achieved during a period of structural change within the Scottish economy. These structural changes are characteristic of most developed economies and comprise the growth and predominance of service sector employment (with growth particularly evident in financial services) and decline in manufacturing.

Thus, notwithstanding some local problems associated with economic restructuring, the vitality of the Scottish macro-economy is at odds with the incidence of poverty in Scotland; problems associated with the macro-economy can be discounted as the over-riding factor explaining why people are poor in Scotland.

Inequality

If the Scottish economy is strengthening and the Scottish economy is one of the strongest in the world, then another possible 'economic' reason for poverty is the distribution of income among the Scottish population. That is, it is possible that poverty prevails not because of macro-economic problems, but rather as a result of the way in which economic gains are shared among the population.

Indeed, as Table 3.3 shows, there has been no significant change in the relative share of overall income between the poorest and the richest in Great Britain.[30] Income shares have been stable for a decade, with the 10 per cent on the lowest income receiving less than 2 per cent of total income, while the 10 per cent on the highest income receive 29 per cent of total income. Significantly, the relative share of overall income has remained constant, despite the recent increases above average earnings of the national minimum wage. More ominously, the recommendation of the Low Pay Commission that the national minimum wage should not now be increased above average earnings does not augur well for a more equitable distribution of income in the UK in the years ahead.[31]

Inequality is clearly a contributory factor to the incidence of poverty in Scotland.

Table 3.3:

Share of total income by the top and bottom 10% of the income distribution (after housing costs and excluding the self-employed), 1994/95, 1999/00, 2004/05, UK

	% share of total income		
	1994/95	**1999/00**	**2004/05**
Bottom 10% of the income distribution	1.7	1.9	1.7
Top 10% of the income distribution	27.7	29.0	29.1
Top 50% of the income distribution	75.1	75.3	74.6

Source: Department for Work and Pensions, *Households Below Average Income*, Corporate Document Services, 2006, Table A3

Conclusion

We have identified four broad multi-faceted factors, which account for the prevalence of poverty in Scotland. Although we should guard against attributing poverty to only social, economic or political factors, and although *some* individuals undoubtedly contribute to their own poverty, the extent of poverty in Scotland suggests that structural explanations are of greater significance in explaining Scotland's poverty. The strength of the Scottish economy, notwithstanding geographical variation and inequalities in the distribution of reward, is such that we cannot reduce poverty to the status of an economic outcome. Thus, political intervention and social factors must be considered. Credit must be given to both the UK government and the Scottish Executive for their commitment to tackling poverty and for the wide-ranging anti-poverty interventions that they have implemented. For those who are satisfied with the rate of progress in tackling poverty, it can be concluded that governments' interventions are now overcoming persistent social problems. On the other hand, the persistence of poverty for some social groups and the enduring barriers to overcoming poverty that their status presents, leads to the conclusion that our governments are not doing enough, quickly enough.

Notes

1 C Philo and J McCormick, 'Poor Places and Beyond: summary findings and policy implications' in C Philo (ed) *Off the Map: the social geography of poverty in the UK*, CPAG, 1993, pp175–188

2 UNISON, 'Single Status and Equal Pay in Local Government', *MSP Briefing* 124, available online at: http://www.unison-scotland.org.uk/briefings/singlestat msp.html

3 Scottish Executive, *Scottish Economic Statistics 2005*, 2005, Table 4.2, p112, available online at: www.scotland.gov.uk/Publications/2005/11/2485808

4 See note 3, Table 4.4, p114

5 See note 3, Table 4.5, p115

6 Department for Work and Pensions, *Opportunity for All: eighth annual report*, The Stationery Office, 2006, available online at: http://www.dwp.gov.uk/ofa/ reports/latest.asp

7 Scottish Executive, *Closing the Opportunity Gap*, available online at: www.scotland.gov.uk/closingtheopportunitygap.

8 Department for Work and Pensions Information Directorate, *Income Support Quarterly Statistics*, online tabulation tool: http://www.dwp.gov.uk/asd/isqse.asp

9 Department for Work and Pensions, *New Deal for Young People and Long-Term Unemployed People aged 25+*, online tabulation tool: http://www.dwp.gov.uk/ asd/ndyp.asp

10 Women's Budget Group, *Women's and Children's Poverty: making the links*, Women's Budget Group, 2005, available online at: www.wbg.org.uk/docu- ments/WBGWomensandchildrenspoverty.pdf

11 J Bradshaw, quoted in Women's Budget Group, *Women's and Children's Poverty: making the links*, Women's Budget Group, 2005, available online at: www.wbg.org.uk/documents/WEGWomensandchildrenspoverty.pdf

12 National Statistics, *Lone Parents in Employment*, 2006, available online at: http://www.statistics.gov.uk/cci/nugget.asp?id=409

13 Department for Work and Pensions, *A New Deal for Welfare: empowering peo- ple to work*, The Stationery Office, 2006

14 National Council for One-parent Families, *One-parent Families Today: the facts*, NCOPF, 2005

15 R St. Clair and others, *Lone Parents in Further Education Colleges*, Scottish Executive, 2005, available online at: www.scotland.gov.uk/Publications/2005/ 11/17154735/47358

16 C Skinner, *How Can Childcare Help to End Child Poverty?*, Joseph Rowntree Foundation, 2006, available online at: www.jrf.org.uk/bookshop/eBooks/ 9781859355053.pdf

17 National Statistics, *Child and Working Tax Credit Statistics*, 2005

18 J Hawksworth, *Universal Early Years Education and Care in 2020: costs, bene- fits and funding options*, Daycare Trust, 2004

19 Help the Aged, *Benefits and Take Up*, Help the Aged, 2006

20 Help the Aged, *Pensions, Pensioner Poverty and the Pension Commission's Final Report*, Help the Aged, 2006

21 F Jones, 'The Effects of Taxes and Benefits on Household Income 2004/05', *Economic Trends* 630, May 2006, Table 4, p61

22 See note 21, Table 3, p59

23 Scottish Executive, *People and Place: regeneration policy statement*, 2006

24 Scottish Executive, *Workforce Plus: an employability framework for Scotland*, 2006

25 Scottish Executive, *More Choices, More Chances: a strategy to reduce the proportion of young people not in education, employment or training in Scotland*, 2006, available online at: http://www.scotland.gov.uk/Publications/2006/06/13100205/0

26 Scottish Executive, *Free Personal Care*, 2006, available online at: http://www.scotland.gov.uk/Topics/Health/care/17655/9334

27 Transport Scotland, *Concessionary Travel*, available online at: http://www.transportscotland.gov.uk/defaultpage1221cde0.aspx?pageID=239; Scottish Parliament, 'The National Bus Travel Concession Scheme for Older and Disabled Persons (Scotland) Order 2006', SI No.107, 2006, available at: http://www.opsi.gov.uk/legislation/scotland/ssi2006/20060107.htm.

28 Scottish Executive, *Scottish Economic Report 2006*, 13th Edition, 2006, available online at: http://www.scotland.gov.uk/Publications/ 2006/06/27171110/0

29 See note 28

30 Jones (see note 21) suggests that income inequality fell between 2000/01 and 2004/05 accounting for this through a small decrease in inequality of original income and the 'progressive' impact of redistributive policies such as the tax credit system and the 2003/04 increase in national insurance contributions (p63). However, it is perhaps too early to attribute too much significance to such small-scale changes; the dominant characteristic is of stability in income inequality in the UK.

31 Low Pay Commission, *National Minimum Wage*, Cm 6759, The Stationery Office, 2006, available online at: www.lowpay.gov.uk/report/pdf/2006_Min_Wage.pdf

Four

Groups vulnerable to poverty

John H McKendrick and John Dickie

This chapter identifies groups that are at particular risk of poverty in Scotland. The risks of poverty are not spread evenly and, as was discussed in the previous chapter, there are many causes of poverty, some of which impact more strongly cn particular groups.

Poverty varies across the life cycle, by family and household type, by social status and according to where we live. This essay describes how poverty varies across each of these four domains for different groups of the population. Children, youth, working-age adults and pensioners are considered for the *life cycle*; lone parents, partnered parents and childless adults are considered for *families and households*; work status, gender, ethnicity and disability are considered for *social status*; and local authorities and urban/rural areas are considered for *place*. The aim of the chapter is to provide information on the likelihood of living in poverty among different groups (risk rate) and of how much of Scotland's poverty is experienced by these groups (poverty composition).

It is important to remember that no group is homogenous and that real people share characteristics across these groupings which may increase or reduce the amount of poverty that they encounter. For example, although children in lone-parent households are, on the whole, at greater risk of experiencing poverty than children in two-parent households (48 per cent of children in lone-parent households are living in poverty, compared with 20 per cent of children in two-parent households – Table 4.2), the risk rate of a child experiencing poverty is far lower in a lone-parent household in which the lone parent works full time, than it is in a couple household in which both adults do not work (13 per cent, compared with 72 per cent – Table 4.2). Similarly, it must also be understood that belonging to one of the groups with a higher at-risk rate of poverty does not in itself cause poverty. As Chapter 3 explained, poverty is caused by the interaction of political, social, economic and personal factors. However, some groups in Scotland are at greater risk of poverty, and this chapter aims to provide key information on these variations.

Where possible, we use Scottish poverty data. Most importantly, this chapter uses the Scottish Executive's analysis of the *Households Below Average Income* (HBAI) data series; this provides a measure of income poverty for children, working-age adults and pensioners in Scotland.[1] However, in the absence of readily available data for Scotland, reference is made to the original HBAI data for Great Britain to describe variation within groups (for example, to identify which groups of children are at greatest risk of experiencing poverty in Scotland).[2] Although using British data to understand poverty in Scotland is not unproblematic, we selectively utilise only that which we consider to provide insight into poverty in Scotland. Finally, we use more broadly-based measures of inequality in Scotland – residential distribution by deprived area status and net household income – to provide further insight. Once again, we use this data carefully, as it does not strictly pertain to poverty, but rather to communities with poverty and low-income living, respectively.

Poverty across the life cycle

Overview

Projections over the next 25 years suggest that the population of Scotland will rise (peaking at just over 5.1 million in 2019) and then slowly decline, falling below 5 million in 2036 and reaching 4.86 million by 2044. This projected growth will reflect recent trends toward an increase in the number of births, a fall in the number of deaths and a rise in the number of people migrating to Scotland.[3] However, the number of people of working age is expected to fall by 7 per cent from 3.18 million in 2004 to 2.96 million in 2031. There will be a steady increase in the number of people of pensionable age, and a decrease in the number of children aged under 16.

People's risk of poverty and the particular barriers to escaping that poverty vary considerably over the life cycle. Children are at highest risk of poverty; many young people continue to face particular disadvantage through exclusion from education, employment or training after school; least progress has been made in reducing poverty among working-age adults; while pensioner poverty has seen the sharpest falls. However, we should avoid over-simplifying poverty to a set of discrete life stages –

Table 4.1:

Age-based variation in populations living in households with below 60 per cent GB median income, after housing costs and including self-employed, Scotland, 1994/05 to 2004/05

Year	Children	Working-age adults	Pensioners	All individuals
	%	%	%	%
1994/95	30	18	29	23
1995/96	32	18	31	23
1996/97	33	19	33	25
1997/98	31	18	28	22
1998/99	31	19	27	23
1999/00	32	20	28	24
2000/01	32	22	25	24
2001/02	31	19	24	22
2002/03	27	20	25	23
2003/04	27	18	21	21
2004/05	24	18	17	19

Source: Scottish Executive, *Scottish Households Below Average Income*, 2004/05, 2006, Table 11

Note: Figures are derived from the *Family Rescurces Survey*. The modified OECD equivalisation scales have been used in the calculations.

experience of poverty at one stage in the life cycle can have a significant impact on an individual's risk of poverty later on.

Table 4.1 illustrates these trends. Pensioner poverty first fell in the mid-1990s, only to stabilise in the late 1990s, before falling again in recent years; 17 per cent of pensioners in Scotland currently experience poverty, almost half the proportion who were in poverty in the mid-1990s. Less dramatic reductions are also evident in child poverty, with the millennium marking a turning point; less than one in every four children in Scotland now live in poverty, compared to one in three in the late 1990s. On the other hand, over the same period, there has been no significant change in the risk of poverty among working-age adults. These figures demonstrate the impact that policy interventions can have on rates of poverty; while children and pensioners have benefited from governments' anti-poverty targets and strategies, those of working age have not.

Children

Despite recent improvements, children are still at significantly greater risk of poverty than either working-age adults or pensioners, with nearly one in four (24 per cent in 2004/05) of Scotland's children growing up in poverty (compared with 18 per cent of working-age adults and 17 per cent of pensioners) (Table 4.1).

However, as Table 4.2 shows, the risk of children experiencing poverty in Great Britain varies hugely on account of family type, number of siblings, the work status of parents or carers, and the age of the mother. Every other child in a lone-parent household experiences poverty (48 per cent), as does every other child in a family with four or more children (50 per cent), and poverty is experienced by almost three-quarters of children in couple households with children in which no adult works (72 per cent).

Higher risks of poverty need to be understood in the context of the overall numbers of children experiencing poverty in Great Britain. Thus, it also important to note that one-half of children in poverty live in households in which an adult is working (50 per cent of children experiencing poverty); and most children experience poverty in households headed by a couple (57 per cent), households with either one or two children (59 per cent) and households with mothers in their 30s (49 per cent) (Table 4.2). Indeed, it is only when households are classified according to the age of youngest child that the risk rate and proportionate share of children experiencing poverty coincide – poverty is clearly more likely to be a characteristic feature of households with young children (Table 4.2).

Young adults

As poverty data tends to be collected at the level of the household, as opposed to the individual, young people's poverty is often concealed by household circumstances. Disentangling young people's circumstances from household circumstances is intriguing; for example, while some young people must remain in the parental home because they cannot afford to move, others whose personal income may be adequate, may be classified as living in poverty, on account of their parents' or carers' circumstances.

Table 4.3 demonstrates that young people in Great Britain are significantly more likely to be living in poverty than older adults of working age (of those without children, 22 per cent of those aged 24 and under are

Table 4.2:
Children's risk of poverty and the share in the proportion of children living in poverty, by household type, Great Britain, 2004/05

	Risk of living in poverty %	Share of the total number of children living in poverty %
Family type		
Lone parent	48	43
Couple	20	57
Family type and work status		
Lone parent, in full-time work	13	2
Lone parent, in part-time work	27	7
Lone parent, not working	72	34
Couple, one or more full-time self-employed	29	12
Couple, both in full-time work	2	1
Couple, one in full-time work, one in part-time work	6	6
Couple, one in full-time work, one not working	21	14
Couple, one or more in part-time work	49	8
Couple, both not in work	72	16
Number of children in household		
1	23	21
2	23	38
3	30	23
4 or more	50	19
Age of mother		
Under 25	41	8
25 to 29	37	14
30 to 34	31	23
35 to 39	26	26
40 to 44	22	18
45 to 49	20	8
50 and over	23	3
Age of youngest child in household		
Under 5	29	43
5 to 10	28	36
11 to 15	24	19
16 to 18	15	2

Source: Department for Work and Pensions, *Households Below Average Income, 2004/05*, Corporate Document Services, 2006, Tables E3.1, E4.1 E5.1, E6.1, 4.5 and 4.8

Note: Poverty is defined as living in a household with less than 60 per cent of contemporary household median income after housing costs.

Figure 4.1:

16–19-year-olds not in education, training or employment by gender, Scotland, 1996–2004

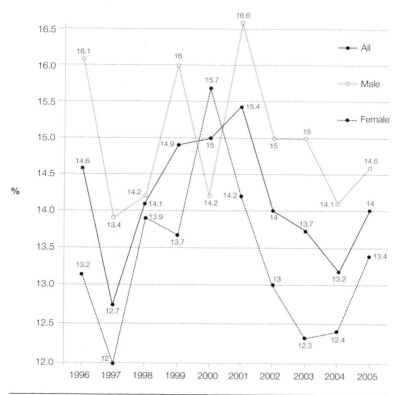

Source: Scottish Executive, *Closing the Opportunity Gap*, Target B. Online tables accessed at http://www.scotland.gov.uk/Topics/People/Social-Inclusion/17415/CtOG-targets/ctog-target-b, 10 May 2006

Note: Data for 1996-2002 is drawn from the *Labour Force Survey*. Data for 2003 is drawn from the *Annual Scottish Labour Force Survey* (Scottish booster to *Labour Force Survey*). Data for 2004 is drawn from the new integrated *Annual Population Survey*.

living in poverty, compared with 12 per cent of those aged 25 to 29; similarly, of those with children, 45 per cent of those aged 24 and under are living in poverty, compared with 32 per cent of those aged 25 to 29).

The primary focus of government concern over young people and poverty is to reduce the numbers who are described as being not in education, training or employment (NEET). Figure 4.1 shows that although there had been a reduction since 2001 in the proportion of young (16–19-year-old) men in Scotland who are NEET, and while the levels of young women who are now NEET have returned to levels experienced in the mid-1990s, following a steady and unwelcome increase in the late 1990s, these positive trends have been arrested for 2005; the number of men and women who are NEET rose between 2004 and 2005. However, caution is urged in interpreting this data; the source survey may not be sensitive enough to infer substantive changes from such small-scale changes in the proportions who are NEET. Unemployed young people make up over half of those categorised as NEET, with a further 44 per cent being categorised as NEET because of disability, sickness or caring responsibilities.[4] The NEET group also includes young people making positive choices to take a gap year between school and university, or to engage in voluntary work. However, others within the NEET group require additional support to engage in education, training or work; estimates suggest that around 20,000 young people are in need of such support.[5] Significant additional barriers are faced by these young people; 28 per cent have no qualifications, 39 per cent have never worked and 14 per cent have a limiting long-term illness.[6]

Working-age adults

Adults of working age in contemporary Scotland are no less likely to be living in poverty, than their counterparts in the mid-1990s (Table 4.1). As for children, risk rates vary among adults of working age and, as was noted in the previous section, risk rates are higher among the youngest adults (Table 4.3).

Table 4.3 also shows that being a parent – and in particular, being a lone parent – and being in a household with less work, is associated with living in poverty for adults of working age in Great Britain. These conclusions are predictable, but the proportion of working-age adults at risk is notable; more than two out of every five lone parents is at risk of living in poverty (44 per cent), while poverty is experienced in more than four out of every five households with children and in which the head of household is unemployed (83 per cent).

Yet, once again, we must guard against reducing our understanding of poverty in Great Britain to the most at-risk groups. More than half of working-age adults living in poverty are from households without children

Table 4.3:

Adults' risk of poverty and the share in the proportion of adults living in poverty, by household type, Great Britain, 2004/05

	Risk of living in poverty %		Share of the total number of adults living in poverty %	
Presence of children in household				
None	16		57	
Some	22		43	
Couple and child status				
Couple, no children	11		21	
Lone man, no children	23		22	
Lone woman, no children	22		14	
Couple, with children	18		30	
Lone parent	44		13	
Work status	**without children**	**with children**	**without children**	**with children**
Single/couple, one or more full-time self-employed	15	26	5	7
Single/couple, all in full-time work	4	3	7	1
Couple, one in full-time work, one in part-time work	4	5	1	3
Couple, one in full-time work, one not working	13	20	4	8
Single/couple, no full-time, one or more in part-time work	24	36	8	7
Workless, head or spouse unemployed	62	83	8	4
Workless, other inactive	43	68	25	15
Age of adult	**without children**	**with children**	**without children**	**with children**
24 and under	22	45	15	4
25 to 29	12	32	5	5
30 to 34	12	23	4	7
35 to 39	15	21	4	10
40 to 44	17	19	4	9
45 to 49	14	17	5	5
50 to 54	13	18	6	2
55 and over	17	17	15	1

Source: Department for Work and Pensions, *Households Below Average Income, 2004/05*, Corporate Document Services, 2006, Tables F4, F6, 5.4, 5.5, 5.7 and 5.8

Note: Poverty is defined as living in a household with less than 60 per cent of contemporary household median income after housing costs.

Table 4.4:

Claimants of state pension and other state support for pensioner client groups, by gender, Scotland, November 2005

	All		Men		Women	
	000s	**%**	**000s**	**%**	**000s**	**%**
SP and PC/MIG, Disabled	125.99	13.1	36.10	10.5	89.89	14.6
SP and PC/MIG, Not disabled	121.78	12.7	38.96	11.4	82.82	13.4
SP but not PC/MIG, Disabled	124.98	13.0	47.88	14.0	77.10	12.5
SP but not PC/MIG, Not disabled	5€9.97	59.4	216.21	63.1	353.76	57.4
PC/MIG but not SP, Disabled	6.74	0.7	1.59	0.5	5.15	0.8
PC/MIG but not SP, Not disabled	4.36	0.5	1.69	0.5	2.67	0.4
Not SP nor PC/MIG, Disabled	3.12	0.3	0.34	0.1	2.78	0.5
Not SP nor PC/MIG, Not disabled	1.92	0.2	0.05	0.1	1.87	0.3
All	958.88		342.82		616.04	

Source: Derived from data sourced from the Department for Work and Pensions tabulation tool (http://www.dwp.gov.uk/asd/tabtool.asp). Data drawn from the Work and Pensions Longitudinal Survey.

Note: Pensioner client groups are based on the combination of benefits being received.

SP = state pension; PC = pension credit; MIG = minimum income guarantee

These client groups have changed since the last edition of *Poverty in Scotland*.

(57 per cent), and one-third of whom are living as a couple (21 per cent of all households living in poverty). One-quarter of working-age adults living in poverty live in households in which at least one adult works and in which there are no children (25 per cent), while a further one-quarter (26 per cent) live in a household with a working adult and children. Similarly, working-age adult poverty is not limited to youth; almost one-quarter of working-age adults living in poverty are in their 40s (23 per cent), with a further one-quarter in their 50s or older (24 per cent).

Pensioners

Almost one million pensioners in Scotland rely on either the state pension or other state support (Table 4.4), almost two-thirds of whom are women.

There has been a decrease in the number of pensioners with incomes below the 60 per cent median threshold, the recognised poverty line. In 2000/01, one-quarter of pensioners in Scotland lived on incomes below this threshold, but by 2004/05 this had dropped to 17 per cent. From being an age-stage group which was more likely to experience poverty, they are now the age-stage at which people are least likely to be poor. Pensioners are, however, still more likely to be persistently poor, with less opportunities to escape their poverty than those of working age.[7]

There is far less variation in risk rate among groups of pensioners in Great Britain, although it is worth noting that the risk of living in poverty is twice as high for pensioner couples with a household head aged 76 and over (22 per cent of whom experience poverty), compared with single men aged under 70 (11 per cent of whom experience poverty). The vast majority of pensioners experiencing poverty are living with their partners (61 per cent).[8]

Families and households

Overview

In addition to demographic population change, social changes also alter the shape of the households in which we live. Among the most significant socio-population changes over the last few decades have been a decrease in family size; a decline in the number of couples who marry; more children being born outside marriage, the majority to cohabiting couples; an increased divorce rate; and growth in the number of lone-parent households.

The number of adults living on their own is expected to increase from 770,000 (34 per cent of all households) in 2004 to over a million (42 per cent) by 2024. The number of lone-parent households is also projected to rise from 150,000 to 200,000, while households containing two or more adults with children is expected to fall from 460,000 (20 per cent of all households) in 2004 to 320,000 (12 per cent) by 2024.[9]

Lone parents

The routes into lone parenthood are many and the characteristics of lone-parent families are varied. There are more than 150,000 lone parents with dependent children in Scotland, one-quarter of all families (24.5 per cent). However, lone parenthood is often not a permanent status, but is rather a

Table 4.5:

Net annual household income by marital status of highest income householder and households type, Scotland, 2003/04

	£0–£6,000	£6,001–£10,000	£10,001–£15,000	£15,001–£20,000	£20,001–£25,000	£25,001–£30,000	£30,001–£40,000	Over £40,000	Base
	%	%	%	%	%	%	%	%	
Marital status of highest income householder									
Married	2	9	15	16	16	15	17	10	14,632
Cohabiting	2	6	13	16	20	18	16	9	2,126
Single/never been married	14	27	31	16	6	3	2	1	5,009
Widowed	21	45	24	7	2	1	0	0	4,272
Divorced	14	32	30	15	6	2	1	1	2,405
Separated	12	24	31	19	8	3	2	0	1,288
All	8	19	21	15	11	9	10	6	29,732
Household type									
Single adult	17	24	28	17	7	3	2	1	4,716
Small adult	4	8	13	16	17	15	16	11	5,029
Single parent	4	29	37	17	7	3	2	1	1,730
Small family	1	4	9	14	18	19	23	12	4,216
Large family	1	4	12	15	16	17	22	13	2,017
Large adult	4	8	14	16	17	15	16	9	2,873
Older smaller	6	23	32	19	10	5	4	2	4,391
Single pensioner	21	47	23	5	2	1	1	0	4,760

Source: C Martin and others, Scotland's People: annual report from the 2003/04 Scottish Household Survey, Scottish Executive, 2006, Tables 6.35 and 6.36

Note: Without identification of the point at which low income reflects poverty, distribution of annual household income date is only a measure of inequality not poverty. Furthermore, the income data in this table is not equivalised. Care has to be taken in interpreting this data when discussing poverty in Scotland.

stage in family life lasting on average around five years.[10] One Plus estimates one-third to one-half of all children in Scotland will spend some time in a lone-parent family. The vast majority of lone parents are women (confirming common understanding), but often the reality of lone parenthood is at odds with some popular perceptions, with most lone parents having separated from a partner and the average age of female lone parents being 35 (contrasting the image of lone parents as single young women).[11]

Only 10 per cent of lone parents are under 25[12] and only one in every seven has never lived with the father of their child.[13]

Lone parents are disproportionately represented among families experiencing poverty in Great Britain. They are more than twice as likely to be poor as compared with couples with children (Table 4.3). Almost half of lone parents are poor (44 per cent).

Evidence from the *Scottish Household Survey* demonstrates that lone parents are disproportionately concentrated at the lower end of the income distribution scale (Table 4.5). Although fewer lone-parent house-holds have an income lower than that of single pensioner households and single adult households (both of which will require less income to experi-ence a comparable standard of living), markedly more lone-parent than two-parent households are concentrated in lower income bands; for example, one-third of lone-parent households in Scotland have an annu-al income of less than £10,000 (33 per cent), compared with one in ten two-parent households (10 per cent).

Partnered parents

Although more lone-parent households experience poverty (Table 4.3) and income levels of lone-parent households are markedly lower than that of two-parent households (Table 4.5), the poverty experienced in two-parent households must not be overlooked. For example, poverty is experienced in one in every five two-parent households in Great Britain in which one parent/carer works and one does not (Table 4.3). Furthermore, almost one-third of the adults living in poverty in Great Britain are from two-par-ent households (30 per cent) – more than twice the number of adults liv-ing in poverty from lone-parent households (13 per cent) (Table 4.3). Thus, although the risk rate of poverty is higher for lone parenthood, there is more poverty in two-parent households in Great Britain.

Social status

Patterns of poverty are not only determined by the stage in life at which we are at, or our family status. Cross-cutting these factors are a range of social factors, which are associated with the likelihood of being poor. Here, we consider the impact of work status, gender, ethnicity and disability.

Workers/non-workers

Those in work in Great Britain are less likely to face poverty. Unsurprisingly, the risk of poverty is lower for households which are 'work-rich' (two-earner couples) than for households which are 'work-poor' (no-earner couples or for couples where part-time work is the only experience) (Table 4.3). Half of the adults of working age who are living in poverty are not in work (52 per cent), with the risk rate of poverty being even more marked – 62 per cent for households in which the head of the household is unemployed and in which there are no children and 83 per cent for households with children and an unemployed head of household.

However, these observations should not be taken to imply that poverty is absent from households with work. After all, almost half of adults of working age who are living in poverty are from households with work (48 per cent). This poverty is spread across a range of household types (defined by work status), with a significant proportion (7–8 per cent) of households in poverty made up of adults of working age in households with children in which one or more adults are self-employed (7 per cent), one adult is engaged in full-time work, while the other does not work (8 per cent); no one is engaged in full-time work, but one or more adults is engaged in part-time work (7 per cent); and in households with no children within which no one is engaged in full-time work, but one or more adults is engaged in part-time work (8 per cent). It is also significant to note that a number of adults experiencing poverty in Great Britain reside in households without children in which all adults are engaged in full-time work (7 per cent). Adult poverty is not solely a result of worklessness (entry into the labour market does not guarantee a route out of poverty) or parental status.

Gender

In Great Britain, more women live in poverty than men, although there is little difference in risk rate between men and women (Table 4.6). This apparent paradox can be explained in that although among pensioners, men are as likely as women to be at risk of poverty (16 per cent and 17 per cent, respectively), many more women than men are living longer, which results in women comprising two-thirds of pensioners living in poverty (65 per cent).

Table 4.6:

Gender variation in risk of poverty and the share in the proportion of people living in poverty, by age group, Great Britain, 2004/05

	Risk of living in poverty %	Share in the total number of people living in poverty %
Working-age adults, individuals		
Men	17	49
Women	19	51
Pensioners, individuals		
Men	16	35
Women	17	65

Source: Department for Work and Pensions, *Households Below Average Income, 2004/05*, Corporate Document Services, 2006, Tables 5.4, 5.7, 6.3 and 6.5

Note: Poverty is defined as living in a household with less than 60 per cent of contemporary household median income after housing costs.

Disability

Having a disability or a limiting long-term illness is associated with impoverished life chances. Table 4.7 shows that although one in five people in Scotland have either a disability and/or a limiting long-term illness (19 per cent), these form almost one-third of people living in Scotland's 20 per cent most deprived areas (29 per cent). There is a consistent negative association between the proportion of people possessing either a disability and/or a limiting long-term illness and the affluence of the area.

The association with disability/long-term illness and most deprived areas is significant, as it is important not to understate the poverty experienced by this group. As Table 4.8 shows, in Great Britain, the risk rate of poverty is significantly greater for those living in most households affected by disability. Exceptions include pensioners; the risk rate of poverty is greater among non-disabled pensioners than disabled pensioners. Nevertheless, the vast majority of adults of working age who are living in poverty are not disabled (69 per cent).

Disability is a particularly significant factor in shaping risk of poverty for those households with at least one disabled adult and at least one disabled child; in these households, the risk of poverty rises to almost two of every five households (37 per cent) (Table 4.8). It is not the presence of

Table 4.7:

Residence of adults with a disability and/or long-term illness, Scotland, 2001/02

	20% most deprived areas	Quintile 2	Quintile 3	Quintile 4	20% least deprived areas	Scotland
	%	%	%	%	%	%
Disability, alone	10	8	6	5	4	7
Long-term illness, alone	12	9	8	6	5	8
Both disability and long-term illness	7	5	4	2	2	4
No disability or long-term illness	71	77	83	87	90	81

Source: Scottish Executive, *Social Focus on Deprived Areas 2005*, 2005, Table 2.16

Table 4.8:

Disabled people's risk of poverty and the share of the proportion of people living in poverty, by age group, Great Britain, 2004/05

	Risk of living in poverty %	Share of the total number of households living in poverty %
Children		
No disabled children	27	88
1 or more disabled child	30	12
Of which, no disabled adult in family	(26)	(6)
Of which, 1 or more disabled adult in family	(37)	(5)
Working-age adults		
No disabled adults	16	69
1 or more disabled adults	28	31
Pensioners		
No disabled pensioners	18	48
1 or more disabled pensioner	16	52

Source: Department for Work and Pensions, *Households Below Average Income, 2004/05*, Corporate Document Services, 2006, Tables 4.4, 4.7, 5.6, 5.9, 6.3 and 6.5

Note: Poverty is defined as living in a household with less than 60 per cent of contemporary household median income after housing costs.

disabled children *per se* that is the most significant factor – households with disabled children and no disabled adults are no more likely to be at risk of income poverty than households without disabled people – but the combination of disability among adults and children is especially significant.

Ethnicity

Information about minority ethnic populations in Scotland is still scarce. The paucity of data is significant, particularly given the small numbers of minority ethnic populations in Scotland and the very different histories of ethnic integration and immigration in Scotland and the rest of the UK.

Table 4.9:
Residence in areas profiled by deprivation, by ethnic group, Scotland, 2001

	Most deprived area	2nd Decile	3rd Decile	4th Decile	5th Decile	6th Decile	7th Decile	8th Decile	9th Decile	Least deprived area
	%	%	%	%	%	%	%	%	%	%
White, Scottish	11	11	10	10	10	10	10	10	10	10
White, Other British	4	4	6	8	10	12	13	13	14	16
White, Irish	13	10	11	10	9	9	9	9	10	11
White, Other	6	6	7	9	8	10	10	12	12	19
Indian	6	6	9	8	8	8	9	12	14	20
Pakistani	11	9	19	8	8	7	7	10	9	11
Bangladeshi	10	11	11	8	9	7	8	10	14	13
South Asian, Other	19	9	9	7	6	7	7	10	12	14
Chinese	8	6	8	8	8	9	8	11	14	20
Caribbean	11	8	11	10	8	10	9	9	9	14
African	21	10	10	10	6	7	8	7	8	14
Black	18	12	11	10	9	8	8	7	6	11
Other Ethnic	13	7	8	8	7	8	8	9	12	19
Any Mixed Background	12	8	10	9	8	8	9	10	11	15

Source: Scottish Executive, *Social Focus on Deprived Areas 2005*, 2005, Table 2.12

Here, we consider the distribution of ethnic groups across deprived areas. Table 4.9 summarises the proportion of households from 14 ethnic groupings across areas classified along a ten-point scale from most deprived to least deprived. Unlike the poverty distributions for other social groupings, there is no striking pattern to emerge that would allow a strong conclusion to be reached on the geography of poverty by ethnicity. Thus, we find that the small populations of African ethnic origin, those of mixed ethnic background, Chinese and South Asians who are not Indian, Pakistani or Bangladeshi are more likely to be over-represented in both the most deprived and the least deprived areas. Over-representation in the least deprived areas is characteristic of those whose ethnic origin is Indian, White British but not Scottish, and Chinese. There would appear to be no striking evidence in Scotland of an ethnic geography to poverty.

On the other hand, data on the risk rate of poverty and composition of people experiencing poverty by ethnic background is available for Great Britain. Here, we find a higher risk rate of poverty among those of minority ethnic origin at each life stage. For example, twice as many pensioners who are of minority ethnic origin are at risk of poverty, compared with those of White ethnic origin (32 per cent, compared with 16 per cent). However, it is important not to over-generalise the experience of poverty among minority ethnic groups. Half of adult individuals (49 per cent) and children (57 per cent) of Pakistani/Bangladeshi ethnic origin are at risk of poverty, compared with around one-third of adult individuals (28 per cent) and children (33 per cent) of Indian ethnic origin. Furthermore, given the very different histories and scale of minority ethnic immigration to Scotland, it cannot be assumed that these British patterns pertain to Scotland. However, in answer to a Parliamentary question it was recently revealed that in Scotland in 2002/03 to 2004/05, after housing costs, an estimated 42 per cent of children with a minority ethnic head of household live in households that experience relative low-income poverty (compared with 24 per cent of children with a non-minority ethnic head of household).[14]

Place

We have already made reference to geographies of poverty in describing the distribution of the population according to ethnicity and disability/ill-

Table 4.10:

Minority ethnic groups' risk of poverty and the share in the proportion of housholds living in povety, by age group, Great Britain, 2004/05

	Risk of living in poverty %	Share of the total number of households living in poverty %
Children		
White	25	80
Mixed	39	1
Asian or Asian British	47	11
Of which, Indian	(33)	(3)
Of which, Pakistani/Bangladeshi	(57)	(7)
Black or Black British	43	5
Chinese or other ethnic group	44	3
Working-age adults		
White	16	82
Mixed	30	1
Asian or Asian British	35	9
Of which, Indian	(28)	(4)
Of which, Pakistani/Bangladeshi	(49)	(5)
Black or Black British	32	4
Of which, Black Caribbean	(24)	(2)
Of which, Black non-Caribbean	(40)	(2)
Chinese or other ethnic group	33	3
Pensioners		
White	16	93
Minority ethnic	32	7

Source: Department for Work and Pensions, *Households Below Average Income, 2004/05*, Corporate Document Services, 2006, Tables 3.3, 3.5, 4.5, 4.7, 5.5, 5.8, 6.3 and 6.5

Note: Poverty is defined as living in a household with less than 60 per cent of contemporary household median income after housing costs.

ness across areas ranked by their deprivation status. To conclude this review of group vulnerability to poverty in Scotland, we now consider the distribution of poverty across local authorities, the urban/rural divide and in local areas.

Local authorities

Over 100,000 adults of working age in Glasgow City claim key benefits (Figure 4.2a), while over 140,000 of the same have been described by the Scottish Executive as 'income deprived' (Table 4.11). When compared to the rest of Scotland, we find that one-fifth of Scotland's poverty is in Glasgow City. Glasgow's poverty is not only extensive, it is also intense. For example, as the definition of a deprived area becomes more stringent, so Glasgow's share of Scotland's deprived area increases; Glasgow has 29 per cent of Scotland's 20 per cent most deprived areas, 34 per cent of Scotland's 15 per cent most deprived areas, 41 per cent of Scotland's 10 per cent most deprived areas and 52 per cent of Scotland's 5 per cent most deprived areas (Table 4.11). Although these figures mark a significant reduction in Glasgow's share of the poverty concentrations since 2004, Glasgow still has a disproportionate share of Scotland's poorest areas.

However, although poverty is most prevalent in Glasgow City, it would be wrong to reduce Scotland's poverty to Glasgow's poverty. Neighbouring North Lanarkshire has over 40,000 claimants of key benefits among adults of working age (20 per cent of its adult population) and almost 54,000 income deprived (17 per cent of the population). Similarly, Glasgow's other neighbouring authorities of West Dunbartonshire, Inverclyde, Renfrewshire and South Lanarkshire are among those in Scotland with the highest rates of key benefit claimants and the highest rates of income poverty. Further exacerbating west coast poverty are the high rates of poverty evident in North and East Ayrshire. Clackmannanshire and Dundee City are the only local authorities on the east coast of Scotland to feature prominently in the 'league table' of the local authorities with more of Scotland's poverty.

It is important to identify the parts of Scotland in which rates of poverty are most prevalent. However, sight must not be lost of local authorities with better than average rates of poverty, but in which reside sizeable numbers of people living in poverty. For example, more people are income deprived in Edinburgh (52,000) and Fife (45,000) than in every other authority in Scotland except for Glasgow and North Lanarkshire (Table 4.11). Aberdeen City and Highland are also authorities with relatively favourable rates of poverty, but high numbers of people experiencing poverty – for example, with 18,000 and 17,000, respectively, of adults of working age claiming key benefits (Figure 4.2a).

The over-concentration of Scotland's poorest areas in Glasgow City (referred to previously) also results in the virtual absence of 'poor areas' in

Figure 4.2a:
Working-age claimants of key benefits, by local authority in Scotland, February 2005

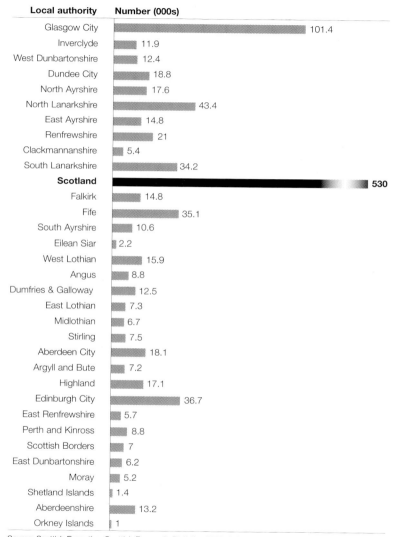

Local authority	Number (000s)
Glasgow City	101.4
Inverclyde	11.9
West Dunbartonshire	12.4
Dundee City	18.8
North Ayrshire	17.6
North Lanarkshire	43.4
East Ayrshire	14.8
Renfrewshire	21
Clackmannanshire	5.4
South Lanarkshire	34.2
Scotland	**530**
Falkirk	14.8
Fife	35.1
South Ayrshire	10.6
Eilean Siar	2.2
West Lothian	15.9
Angus	8.8
Dumfries & Galloway	12.5
East Lothian	7.3
Midlothian	6.7
Stirling	7.5
Aberdeen City	18.1
Argyll and Bute	7.2
Highland	17.1
Edinburgh City	36.7
East Renfrewshire	5.7
Perth and Kinross	8.8
Scottish Borders	7
East Dunbartonshire	6.2
Moray	5.2
Shetland Islands	1.4
Aberdeenshire	13.2
Orkney Islands	1

Source: Scottish Executive, *Scottish Economic Statistics 2005*, 2005, Table 5.3

Note: Key benefits are jobseeker's allowance, incapacity benefit, severe disability allowance, disability living allowance and income support. This table is drawn from a small sample of cases.

*Great care should be taken in interpreting data, as this figure is based on a small number of cases.

Figure 4.2b:
Working-age claimants of key benefits, by local authority in Scotland, February 2005

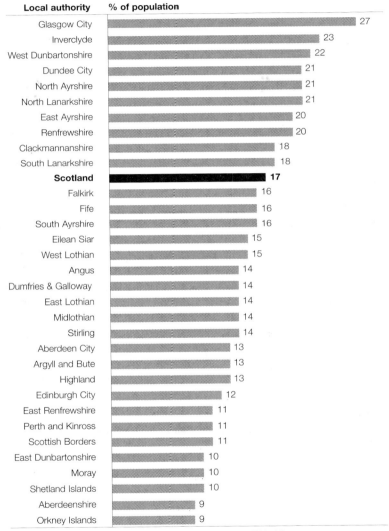

Local authority	% of population
Glasgow City	27
Inverclyde	23
West Dunbartonshire	22
Dundee City	21
North Ayrshire	21
North Lanarkshire	21
East Ayrshire	20
Renfrewshire	20
Clackmannanshire	18
South Lanarkshire	18
Scotland	**17**
Falkirk	16
Fife	16
South Ayrshire	16
Eilean Siar	15
West Lothian	15
Angus	14
Dumfries & Galloway	14
East Lothian	14
Midlothian	14
Stirling	14
Aberdeen City	13
Argyll and Bute	13
Highland	13
Edinburgh City	12
East Renfrewshire	11
Perth and Kinross	11
Scottish Borders	11
East Dunbartonshire	10
Moray	10
Shetland Islands	10
Aberdeenshire	9
Orkney Islands	9

Source: Scottish Executive, *Scottish Economic Statistics 2005*, 2005, Table 5.3

Note: Key benefits are jobseeker's allowance, incapacity benefit, severe disability allowance, disability living allowance and income support. This table is drawn from a small sample of cases.

*Great care should be taken in interpreting data, as this figure is based on a small number of cases.

more rural authorities. For example, while 2.4 per cent of Scotland's income deprived live in Aberdeenshire, just over 0.6 per cent of Scotland's 20 per cent most deprived areas are found in the authority (Table 4.11). The dispersion of poverty – the hidden poverty without place – is most striking for Eilean Siar. Although the proportion of income deprived is marginally above the average for Scotland (14.3 per cent, compared with 13.9 per cent for Scotland), none of Scotland's 20 per cent most deprived areas are found in this authority.

The poverty of place also cannot be reduced to discrete macro-geographies of affluence and poverty. Although a disproportionate share of Scotland's poverty is found in Glasgow City and neighbouring authorities, these swathes of poverty sit alongside East Dunbartonshire and East Renfrewshire, two of the authorities in Scotland in which poverty is least prevalent – for example, just over 7 per cent of working-age adults are income deprived in these authorities, compared with almost 25 per cent of those from Glasgow City.

Urban and rural

As the discussion of poverty across Scotland's local authorities emphasises, poverty is most prevalent in urban settings. Table 4.12 emphasises that almost half of Scotland's 750,000 income deprived live in large urban areas (48 per cent) and more than one-quarter live in smaller urban areas (29 per cent).

However, the urban basis of Scotland's poverty, should not disguise the fact that poverty is also prevalent in rural Scotland. Almost 100,000 people in rural Scotland are income deprived, amounting to one in ten of the rural population. Chapter 18 explores the phenomenon of rural poverty in some detail. Sight must also not be lost of the fact that one-quarter of Scotland's poor live between the extremes of city and country – one in eight people in small towns (accessible and remote) experience poverty in Scotland.

Conclusion

This chapter has highlighted how the risk of poverty for people in Scotland is related to their age, the kinds of households they live in, their social sta-

Table 4.11:
Area-based poverty, local authorities in Scotland, February 2005

Local authority	Population		Deprived areas (data zones) in Scotland – local authority share of Scottish total			
	% of population who are income deprived	No. of income deprived	5% most deprived areas %	10% most deprived areas %	15% most deprived areas %	20% most deprived areas %
Glasgow City	24.7	142,915	52.0	41.3	33.8	28.5
West Dunbartonshire	19.6	17,930	1.5	2.6	3.4	3.1
Inverclyde	19.2	15,850	4.0	4.5	4.3	3.8
Dundee City	18.6	26,335	4.0	6.0	5.4	5.2
North Ayrshire	17.3	23,530	2.8	3.5	3.4	3.7
East Ayrshire	16.7	20,015	2.5	2.6	2.9	3.1
North Lanarkshire	16.7	53,795	5.2	6.8	8.6	10.2
Clackmannanshire	15.3	7,390	0.6	1.4	1.5	1.3
Renfrewshire	14.9	25,355	2.8	3.4	3.7	4.6
Eilean Siar	14.3	3,765	0	0	0	0
Scotland	**13.9**	**707,728**				
South Lanarkshire	13.8	42,200	4.0	5.7	5.7	6.1
South Ayrshire	13.1	14,600	1.5	1.2	1.3	1.6
Falkirk	12.9	19,085	0.3	1.7	1.9	2.2
West Lothian	12.8	20,670	0.3	0.5	1.4	2.3
Fife	12.6	44,645	1.5	3.4	4.8	6.1
Dumfries & Galloway	11.6	17,510	0.6	0.9	1.1	1.2
Angus	11.5	12,495	0	0.2	0.8	0.7
Edinburgh City	11.4	51,685	8.3	7.1	6.5	5.8
Highland	11.3	23,875	0.9	1.2	1.7	1.8
Midlothian	11.1	8,870	0	0.2	0.5	0.8
Aberdeen City	10.8	22,025	2.8	2.8	2.8	2.8
Argyll and Bute	10.6	9,630	0.6	0.6	1.0	0.8
East Lothian	10.1	9,210	0	0	0.1	0.2
Stirling	10.0	8,615	1.5	0.8	0.7	0.8
Moray	9.3	8,170	0	0	0	0.2
Scottish Borders	9.3	10,170	0.3	0.3	0.3	0.5
Perth and Kinross	9.2	12,340	0.6	0.8	0.9	0.8
Shetland Islands	8.8	1,930	0	0	0	0
Orkney Islands	7.8	1,525	0	0	0	0
East Renfrewshire	7.5	6,685	0.3	0.2	0.3	0.6
Aberdeenshire	7.4	17,115	0.6	0.3	0.6	0.6
East Dunbartonshire	7.3	7,820	0.3	0.3	0.3	0.5

Source: Scottish Executive, *Scottish Index of Multiple Deprivation 2006*, 2006, Tables 1.4 and 2.9

Table 4.12:
Income deprivation in urban and rural areas, Scotland, 2004

	No. of income deprived	% of population who are income deprived	% of income-deprived people in 15% most deprived areas	% of local areas (data zones) in 15% most deprived areas
Large urban	363,934	18.5	58.0	27.7
Other urban	216,357	14.9	28.2	12.1
Accessible small towns	63,322	12.4	13.0	5.1
Remote small towns	19,593	13.9	17.4	7.9
Accessible rural	65,209	9.2	8.9	2.5
Remote rural	28,799	9.9	2.2	0.5
Scotland	757,214	15.0	38.3	15.0

Source: Scottish Executive, *Social Focus on Deprived Areas 2005*, 2005, Tables 1.11

tus and the places in which they live. Marked and important variations are apparent, depending on these factors. However, it is also clear that poverty impacts on people to a greater or lesser extent regardless of how old they are, who they live with, their gender, ethnicity, work status or geographical location. It is, therefore, important to examine the risk of poverty alongside the overall proportion of the population who make up these different groups and places – the people and places with the highest risk of poverty do not necessarily account for the greatest numbers of people living in poverty.

Notes

1 Scottish Executive, *Scottish Households Below Average Income, 2004/05*, 2006

2 Department for Work and Pensions, *Households Below Average Income, 2004/05*, Corporate Document Services, 2006

3 Registrar General for Scotland, *Mid-2005 Population Estimates Scotland: population estimates by sex, age and administrative area*, National Statistics, 2006, available online at: http://www.gro-scotland.gov.uk/statistics/library/mid-2005-population-estimates/index.html

4 Scottish Executive, *More Choices, More Chances: a strategy to reduce the proportion of young people not in education, employment or training in Scotland*,

2006, available online at: http://www.scotland.gov.uk/Publications/2006/06/13100205/16

5 See note 4

6 See note 4

7 Help the Aged, *Attitudes to Pensioners and Pensioner Poverty*, Briefing Paper, 2006, available online at: http://policy.helptheaged.org.uk/_policy/Poverty/Pensions/_default.htm

8 See note 2, Tables G3.1 and G5.1

9 Registrar General for Scotland, *Scotland's Population 2005: the Registrar General's annual review of demographic trends*, National Statistics, 2006, available online at: http://www.gro-scotland.gov.uk/statistics/library/annrep/rgs-annual-review-2005/chapter-1/chapter-1-demographic-overview-households.html

10 One Plus, *Statistics*, 2006, available online at: http://www.oneplus.org/policy-and-campaigns/statistics

11 See note 10

12 One Parent Families Scotland, *General Statistics*, One Parent Families Scotland, 2006, available online at: http://www.opfs.org.uk/factfile/stats01.html

13 One Parent Families, *One Parent Families Today: the facts*, One Parent Families, 2005

14 Scottish Parliament, *Written Answers*, 28 March 2006, available online at: http://www.scottish.parliament.uk/business/pqa/wa-06/wa0328.htm

Five
Living in poverty
Lynn Burnett and John H McKendrick

This chapter considers the experience of living in poverty in contemporary Scotland, one of the wealthiest countries in the world. It focuses on the here and now. It does not speculate on the long-term consequences of being poor, or claim that people currently experiencing poverty will be for evermore condemned to a life of adversity. It is a chapter about how poverty is understood and experienced by 'the poor'.

The chapter draws upon qualitative and quantitative data to capture the intensity of personal experience and to describe the common life experiences shared among those living in poverty. Although not the only recent qualitative study in Scotland to capture the experiences of people living in poverty,[1] it draws exclusively from Scottish findings from the Get Heard project, a UK initiative through which people with first-hand experience of poverty expressed their opinions on government policies designed to combat poverty.[2] Although Get Heard does not capture all of the voices of people experiencing poverty in Scotland,[3] it testifies to the prevalence and injustice of poverty in some of its most pervasive manifestations: the lack of finance in a consumer society, a lack of belonging and lack of control, poor physical health, a lack of genuine participation, and an impoverished community life and local environment. These five themes structure the account that follows. To bolster these insights, the chapter draws selectively from national survey data to provide an understanding of the prevalence of life experiences among those living in poverty in contemporary Scotland.

Money

> 'Poverty is being skint.'[4]

According to people experiencing poverty, a lack of money leads to social exclusion in contemporary Scotland. For people living on a low income, a lack of money leads to a fragile existence that involves the threat of falling into debt, being forced to choose between one necessity and another, going without, being caught frequently in a cycle of 'dead-end' jobs, and being unable to save money.

The insecurity associated with a lack of money shapes every other aspect of one's life. Words such as 'frustrated' or 'desperate', and phrases such as 'juggling all the balls in the air', or 'poverty is about lack of choice' saturate the language of people struggling to get by on a low income. It is also practically impossible to accumulate savings while experiencing poverty, further exacerbating the instability of people living in the most fragile of circumstances.

National survey data reinforce these conclusions. As Table 5.1 shows, households in Scotland with the lowest net income are most likely not to have a bank account and are least likely to have any savings or investments. Thus, while virtually all households with an annual net income over £20,000 have a bank or building society account, one in every six of the households with a household income of less than £6,000 do not possess such an account. Similarly, one in two households with an annual income of less than £15,000 have no savings or investments. An unacceptable and disproportionate share of people living in poverty in Scotland do not have the financial means that lend themselves towards stability and that enable them to fend off unforeseen financial crises.

It should come as no surprise, therefore, that debt was one of the most highlighted themes in the Get Heard workshops as people spoke of the ease of falling into debt, the prevalence of loan sharks, poor financial education, and the stigma attached to being in debt. This confirmed the findings of a recent Scottish Executive-funded study, which demonstrated that most people experiencing poverty are ashamed of being in debt, and that those who owe money on major household bills acknowledge their debt and, therefore, their obligations to creditors – their situation is one of 'can't pay' rather than 'won't pay'.[5]

The vicious spiralling circle of debt – wherein high-cost credit must be used to stave off existing debt – is not the only way in which people experiencing poverty encounter difficulties in overcoming their financial problems. Living on a low income is also associated with less ready access to those resources which are important to participate fully in contemporary Scotland, including accessing the world of work. As Table 5.2 shows, households in Scotland with the lowest net income are most likely not to have home internet access and access to a car for private use. Thus, two-thirds of households with an annual net income less than

Table 5.1:

Financial resources by net annual household income, Scotland, 2003/04

	£0 – £6,000	£6,001 – £10,000	£10,001 – £15,000	£15,001 – £25,000	£20,001 – £25,000	£25,001 – £30,000	£30,001 – £40,000	Over £40,000	Scotland
	%	%	%	%	%	%	%	%	%
Respondent or partner has bank or building society account									
Yes	81	82	89	94	97	97	97	99	91
No	15	15	9	3	1	0	0	0	7
Refused to say	4	3	2	3	2	2	2	1	3
Base	2,566	5,697	6,126	4,338	3,429	2,772	3,063	1,741	29,732
Respondent or partner has any savings or investments									
Yes	39	40	46	55	61	68	74	85	54
No	52	53	47	38	32	25	19	11	39
Refused to say	8	6	6	6	6	6	7	3	6
Don't know	1	0	0	1	1	1	1	1	1
Base	2,566	5,697	6,126	4,338	3,429	2,772	3,063	1,741	29,732
Amount of savings or investments in households with savings and investments									
Under £1,000	29	28	27	23	19	16	10	5	20
£1,000 – £4,999	25	30	27	27	27	28	26	26	26
£5,000 – £9,999	13	16	15	13	19	17	21	14	16
£10,000 – £15,999	9	9	9	10	10	13	12	13	11
£16,000 – £29,999	9	7	9	10	9	9	13	16	10
£30,000 – £74,999	8	7	9	10	9	10	10	17	10
£75,000 or more	8	4	4	6	8	8	9	21	8
Base	684	1,653	2,111	1,766	1,585	1,353	1,633	1,198	11,983

Source: C Martin and others, *Scotland's People: Annual Report from the 2003/04 Scottish Household Survey*, Scottish Executive, 2005, Tables 6.47, 6.38 and 6.43

Note: Without identification of the point at which low income reflects poverty, distribution of household income data is only a measure of inequality not poverty. Furthermore, the income data in this table is not equivalised. Care has to be taken in interpreting this data when discussing poverty in Scotland.

£10,000 do not have access to a car for private use (compared with less than one in ten households with an annual income of over £20,000) and only one in every six households with a net household income of less than

Table 5.2:

Aspects of consumption by net annual household income, Scotland, 2003/04

	£3,000 – £6,000	£6,001 – £10,000	£10,001 – £15,000	£15,001 – £20,000	£20,001 – £25,000	£25,001 – £30,000	£30,001 – £40,000	Over £40,000	Scotland
	%	%	%	%	%	%	%	%	%
Cars available for private use									
Yes	35	36	55	77	90	95	97	98	67
No	65	64	45	23	10	5	3	2	33
Base	*2,566*	*5,697*	*6,126*	*4,338*	*3,429*	*2,772*	*3,063*	*1,741*	*29,732*
Home internet access									
Yes	17	16	27	46	59	70	82	89	44
No	83	84	73	54	41	30	18	11	56
Base	*2,566*	*5,697*	*6,126*	*4,338*	*3,429*	*2,772*	*3,063*	*1,741*	*29,732*

Source: C Martin and others, *Scotland's People: Annual Report from the 2003/04 Scottish Household Survey*, Scottish Executive, 2005, Tables 6.3, 6.22 and 6.43

Note: See Table 5.1

£10,000 have home internet access, compared with the majority of households with an annual income of over £20,000.

Children feel the consequences of their parent(s)'/guardian(s)' limited income, for example, by encountering difficulties in keeping pace with their peers in fashion or leisure. Poverty for people in Scotland begins with a lack of income but it is not solely concerned with the basic necessities of existence, such as having a roof over one's head or food on the table. If young people are accepted by their peers partly on account of their clothing and participation in leisure, then those children whose parents are unable to afford these social necessities will find it more difficult to be accepted and included.

If we step back to consider the basic necessities of existence, then we find unacceptable deprivations among Scotland's poorest people. As Table 5.3 shows, fuel poverty is almost absent among households in Scotland with a net weekly income of over £300. In sharp contrast, almost three-quarters of those households with a net weekly income of less than

Table 5.3:
Fuel poverty and extreme fuel poverty by household income, Scotland, 2002

Weekly net household income[2]	Fuel poverty[1]			Extreme fuel poverty[1]		
	000s	% fuel poverty within household income band		000s	% extreme fuel poverty within household income band	
Less than £100	86	72		40	33	
£100 – £199.99	159	28		24	4	
£200 – £299.99	29	6		*	1	
£300 – £399.99	8	2		*	0	
£400 – £499.99	*	1		*	0	
£500 – £699.99	*	0		*	0	
£700 or more	*	0		*	0	

Source: D Cormack and others, *Fuel Poverty in Scotland: further analysis of the Scottish House Condition Survey,* Communities Scotland, 2004, Tables 2.10 and 2.17

Notes:

1. The definition of fuel poverty that is used is that specified by the Scottish Executive in the Fuel Poverty Statement of 2002. Households are defined as 'fuel poor' if they would be required to spend more than 10 per cent of household income on fuel. Households in extreme fuel poverty would be required to spend more than 20 per cent of their household income on fuel. For a more detailed discussion, see D Cormack and others, *Fuel Poverty in Scotland: further analysis of the Scottish House Condition Survey*, Communities Scotland, 2004.

2. See Table 5.1

£100 experience fuel poverty, as do one in every four households with a net weekly household income of between £100 and £199.

Belonging and control

'Your worth is all about money, money, money.'

The problems caused by poverty extend far beyond the ability to consume, with people living in poverty sensing that their worth is often rated (adversely) on economic terms. Being seen to be poor is to be seen to be less worthy, and leads to low self-esteem and social isolation. People living on a low income experience stigmatisation on account of their poverty,

Table 5.4:

Mental distress and psychological ill-health across equivalised household income[1] quintile, by age/sex profile, Scotland, 2003

	20% lowest income household	Quintile 2	Quintile 3	Quintile 4	20% highest income household
	%	%	%	%	%
Psychological well-being among adults					
Men, GHQ12 of zero	55	62	68	72	73
Women, GHQ12 of zero	49	59	61	65	62
Psychological well-being among children, aged 13 to 15[2]					
Boys, GHQ12 of zero	79	72	69	77	66
Girls, GHQ12 of zero	65	65	59	68	80
Psychological well-being among children, aged 4 to 12[3]					
Boys, SDQ of 0–13	69	70	87	86	94
Girls, SDQ of 0–13	77	81	88	89	95

Source: C Bromley and others, *Scottish Health Survey 2003, Volumes 2 and 3*, Scottish Executive, 2005, Table 6.14

Notes:

1. Although income data is equivalised, without identification of the point at which low income reflects poverty, distribution of household income data is only a measure of inequality not poverty. Care has to be taken in interpreting this data when discussing poverty in Scotland.

2. As described by Gray and Leyland in C Bromley and others, *Scottish Health Survey 2003, Volumes 2 and 3*, Scottish Executive, 2005, 'The General Health Questionnaire (GHQ12) was used to assess psycho-social health. The GHQ12 is a standard measure of mental distress and psychological ill-health, consisting of 12 questions on recent concentration abilities, sleeping patterns, self-esteem, stress, despair, depression, and confidence. Responses to these items were scored, with one point given each time a particular feeling or type of behaviour was reported to have been experienced 'more than usual' or 'much more than usual' over the past few weeks. These scores are combined to create an overall score of between zero and twelve. A score of four or more (referred to as a 'high' GHQ12 score) has been used here to indicate the presence of a possible psychiatric disorder. A score of zero on the GHQ12 questionnaire could, in contrast, be considered to be an indicator of psychological well-being. (p135)

3. As described by Gray and Leyland in C Bromley and others, *Scottish Health Survey 2003, Volumes 2 and 3*, Scottish Executive, 2005, 'Since the GHQ12 is self-completion it is not recommended for younger children. Instead the Strengths and Difficulties Questionnaire (SDQ) was answered by parents on behalf of children 4-12 years. The SDQ comprises 25 questions covering aspects such as consideration, hyperactivity, malaise, mood, sociability, obedience, anxiety, and unhappiness. These can be condensed into five component symptom scores corresponding to emotional symptoms, conduct problems, hyperactivity, peer problems and prosocial behaviour, ranging in value from zero to ten. A total SDQ score (referred to here as a total deviance score) was calculated by summing the scores from each domain, with the exception of pro-social behaviour, ranging from zero to forty. For each, values can be classified as normal, borderline and abnormal.' (p135)

a lack of emotional and practical support that could be provided by those in more powerful positions, and a feeling of being unable to participate fully in one's community.

Poverty strips people of their dignity. Get Heard participants consistently remarked on their feelings of inadequacy when facing support agencies and services designed by people in powerful positions. People often feel deprived of the respect to which they should be entitled as human beings, and perceive that they are shunned by the public through media misrepresentation, which promotes an understanding that the poor only have themselves to blame for their poverty. It is difficult for people to feel they belong when their lives are rationalised through misleading stereotypes, paying little regard to individual circumstance and need. People want, and are entitled to, personalised 'no strings attached' attention that values them as human beings.

Figure 5.1:

Life expectancy and healthy life expectancy[1] by sex and deprivation area quintiles, Scotland, 2000

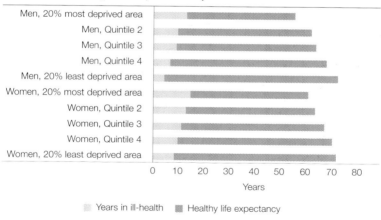

Source: D Clark and others, *Healthy Life Expectancy in Scotland*, HLE Measurement in Scotland Steering Group, 2004, Tables 5.22 and 5.23

Notes:

1. Uses 'self-reported health' as a measure of ill-health.

2. The table presents area data, which will not coincide absolutely with low-income households (and households living in poverty). Furthermore, without identification of the point at which these quintiles reflects poverty, distribution of household income data is only a measure of inequality not poverty. Care has to be taken in interpreting this data when discussing poverty in Scotland.

Mental well-being is, not surprisingly, less than satisfactory among the poorest people in Scotland. Table 5.4 reports findings of psychological health using standard measurement tools from the Scottish Health Survey; as the notes explain, the *lower* the score, the *more* likely it is that psychological well-being is evident. For adults, there are interesting gender differences – men's mental health improves steadily as household income level rises, whereas for women, there is a sharp difference between women living in households with the very lowest household income levels (lowest 20 per cent) and all others – although, the key conclusion is that mental distress is most prevalent in low-income households (for both men and women). Of equal concern is the finding that mental distress is more prevalent among young boys and girls living in low-income households, suggesting that the strains of low-income living do not only impair the quality of life of adults. For older children – young teenagers of between 13 and 15 – the findings are more complex; boys from households with the lowest income levels express the highest levels of psychological well-being, and girls from households with the lowest income levels express higher levels of psychological well-being than girls from middle-income households. This 'anomaly' begs further study, but should not detract from the overarching conclusion that low-income living is associated with higher levels of mental distress.

Physical health

'Poverty is about not being able to feed yourself properly.'

Men and women who do not live in poverty live longer and enjoy more years in good health (Figure 5.1). The harsh realities of life expectancy statistics and healthy life expectancy statistics make for unpalatable reading. Men in the poorest places in Scotland can expect to spend over 13 of their 69 years in ill-health, compared to men in the most affluent places who can expect to spend just over four of their 78 years in ill-health. Although women live longer, they can also expect to spend more years than men in ill-health. Thus, women in the poorest places in Scotland can expect to spend almost 15 of their 76 years in ill-health, compared with women in the most affluent places who can expect to spend just over eight of their 81 years in ill-health. Indeed, expressed as area statistics, these figures most probably underestimate the different life experiences and expectancies of Scotland's rich, comfortable and poor.

Clearly, poverty prevents men and women from enjoying healthy lifestyles. Although programmes do exist throughout Scotland to promote healthy eating and exercise among the poor, people experiencing poverty are not always able to access these services for want of money or time. For example, the Get Heard research uncovered a sense of frustration among Scotland's poor over government promotion of five portions of fruit and vegetables per day, while not providing sufficient money to enable them to purchase such a healthy diet.

There is evidence that men and women living in households with the lowest income are living less healthy lifestyles than those in the most afflu-ent households.[6] Comparing the most and least affluent households (high-est 20 per cent [HIH] and lowest 20 per cent [LIH] by net household income), we find that rates of smoking are higher in the lowest than the highest income households (for example, 51 per cent for men in the LIH compared with 15 per cent for men in the HIH), whereas levels of physi-cal activity are lower (for example, 26 per cent of women in the LIH meet the recommended level, compared with 33 per cent of women in the HIH) and consumption of five daily portions of fruits and vegetables is lower (for example, 16 per cent of men in the LIH, compared with 28 per cent of men in the HIH). Likewise, exposure to nicotine is higher and consump-tion of fruit and vegetables is lower for children from the LIH. However, children in the LIH are as, if not more, likely than children in the HIH to meet the current recommendations for physical activity levels. Furthermore, and in sharp contrast to the public persona of people expe-riencing poverty, consumption of alcohol above recommended levels is lower for both men and women from the LIH (for example, 11 per cent of women in the LIH consume in excess of recommended intake, compared with 20 per cent of women in the HIH).

On the whole, however, people experiencing poverty are living a less healthy lifestyle than their more affluent counterparts. These inequities are not surprising; people living on low incomes and facing the day-to-day struggles of simply making ends meet are less able to have the time, ener-gy or financial resources to live the healthiest of lifestyles.

Neither should it be surprising that both adults and children living on the lowest incomes in Scotland experience less favourable health out-comes (Tables 5.5 and 5.6). As Table 5.5 shows for both men and women, low-income living is associated with fewer people assessing their health to be 'very good' (for example, 57 per cent of women in the LIH, compared with 88 per cent of women in the HIH), higher annual accident rates (for example, 31 per cent of men in the LIH, compared with 18 per cent of

Table 5.5:

Selected health outcomes for adults across equivalised household income quintile,[1] by age/sex profile, Scotland, 2003

	20% lowest income household	Quintile 2	Quintile 3	Quintile 4	20% highest income household
	%	%	%	%	%
Obesity (Body Mass Index over 30)					
Men	16.5	25.1	23.6	26.1	20.3
Women	28.8	31.8	29.4	22.1	22.9
General health self-assessed as very good					
Men	58	62	74	83	88
Women	57	64	71	84	88
Annual accident rates for 16–44-year-olds					
Men	31	29	19	23	18
Women	18	14	16	14	11
Respiratory symptoms					
Men, wheezed in the last 12 months	24	23	18	13	12
Men, doctor diagnosed asthma	13	13	12	10	12
Women, wheezed in the last 12 months	24	20	16	10	11
Women, doctor diagnosed asthma	16	14	15	11	13
High blood pressure					
Men	30.2	31.8	32.5	33.4	30.0
Women	35.3	33.5	33.4	27.3	29.3
Doctor diagnosed diabetes					
Men	5.1	6.1	3.1	2.6	2.8
Women	5.3	3.8	3.7	2.2	3.4

Source: C Bromley and others, *Scottish Health Survey 2003, Volume 2*, Scottish Executive, 2005, Tables 5.11, 6.8, 7.4, 8.7, 9.4 and 10.4

Note: See Note 1, Table 5.4

men in the HIH), higher incidence of respiratory problems (for example, 24 per cent of men in the LIH wheezed in the last 12 months, compared with 12 per cent of men in the HIH) and higher levels of diabetes (for example, 5.3 per cent of women in the LIH, compared with 3.4 per cent of women

Table 5.6:

Selected health outcomes for children across equivalised household income quintiles, by sex or age, Scotland, 2003

	20% lowest income household	Quintile 2	Quintile 3	Quintile 4	20% highest income household
	%	%	%	%	%
Overweight (including obese)					
Boys	30.0	37.3	35.4	36.8	35.1
Girls	31.7	34.9	27.1	27.5	26.0
General health self-assessed as very good					
Boys	86	90	94	95	98
Girls	90	93	97	97	97
Annual accident rates					
0–5-year-olds	19	17	17	13	14
6–10-year-olds	20	25	14	14	17
11–15-year-olds	30	22	20	17	24
Respiratory symptoms among 0–6-year-olds					
Boys, wheezed in the last 12 months	21	22	14	10	12
Boys, doctor diagnosed asthma	21	16	16	12	8
Girls, wheezed in the last 12 months	14	20	13	8	8
Girls, doctor diagnosed asthma	13	14	6	7	2

Source: C Bromley and others, *Scottish Health Survey 2003, Volume 2*, Scottish Executive, 2005, Tables 5.9, 6.8, 7.4 and 8.9

Note: See Note 1, Table 5.4

in the HIH). Furthermore, women in the LIH are more likely than those from the HIH to exhibit high blood pressure (35 per cent, compared with 29 per cent) and are more likely to be obese (29 per cent, compared with 23 per cent). More positively, men in the LIH are no more likely than men from more affluent households to experience high blood pressure and they are less likely to be obese than men from more affluent households. Similar patterns across household income levels and gender are evident for children (Table 5.6).

Community life and environment

'There is no chance for people like us to make improvements in our lives.'

Get Heard participants continually spoke about the importance of living and working locally, finding worthwhile employment, of knowing one's neighbours and feeling safe in one's community. People experiencing poverty are more likely to be living in deprived areas with inadequate services and facilities; their physical environments are often badly cared for and 'depressing', and they are more likely to feel unsafe in their neighbourhood.

Table 5.7 uses information from the Scottish Household Survey to compare perceptions of night-time safety at home and in the wider neighbourhood. On the whole, the majority of people in Scotland perceive themselves to be safe in their own homes at night, and there is little significant difference in the proportion who feel unsafe between higher income households and lower income households. However, there is a subtle difference to be discerned; those from the lowest income households (earning less than £10,000 per year) are less likely to feel that they are very safe in their homes at night (for example, 68 per cent of those earning less than £6,000 per year, compared with a Scottish average of 75 per cent). More marked differences between those living in low- and high-income households are evident with regard to perceived safety in the wider neighbourhood at night. Almost one in seven (13 per cent) of those living in households with the lowest income (less than £6,000 per year) feel not at all safe in their neighbourhood, compared with only 2 per cent of the households with the highest income (over £40,000 per year) and the Scottish average of 8 per cent.

Local area differences extend beyond perceptions of safety. As Table 5.8 shows, people living in the most deprived areas of Scotland (the areas with a disproportionate share of people experiencing poverty in Scotland) are more likely to express displeasure over problems in their neighbourhood (21 per cent are concerned with vandalism and 18 per cent with drug abuse in their neighbourhood). On the other hand, although people living in deprived areas are less likely to express pleasure over noise and aesthetics, they are more likely to comment favourably on their area with regard to neighbours and public transport.

In broader environmental terms, deprived areas are also more likely to be in the vicinity of polluted and derelict sites.

Table 5.7:

Perceptions of personal safety by net annual household income,[1] Scotland, 2003/04

	£0 – £6,000	£6,001 – £10,000	£10,001 – £15,000	£15,001 – £20,000	£20,001 – £25,000	£25,001 – £30,000	£30,001 – £40,000	Over £40,000	Scotland
	%	%	%	%	%	%	%	%	%
How safe respondent feels at home at night									
Very safe	68	69	72	76	77	79	82	82	75
Fairly safe	28	26	23	20	21	18	16	15	21
Not particularly	3	3	3	3	2	2	1	2	2
Not at all	1	1	1	1	1	0	0	1	1
Don't know	1	0	0	0	0	0	0	Neg[2]	0
Base	2,468	5,495	5,831	4,030	3,127	2,468	2,730	1,562	27,711
How safe respondent feels walking alone in the neighbourhood at night									
Very safe	28	27	29	37	39	43	44	49	36
Fairly safe	36	35	37	38	38	39	40	38	37
Not particularly	17	19	17	15	15	12	11	11	15
Not at all	13	12	11	7	5	5	3	2	8
Don't know	7	7	6	4	3	2	2	1	4
Base	2,468	5,495	5,831	4,030	3,127	2,468	2,730	1,562	27,711

Source: C Martin and others, *Scotland's People: Annual Report from the 2003/04 Scottish Household Survey*, Scottish Executive, 2005, Tables 4.60 and 4.66

Notes:

1. See Table 5.1

2. Negative describes cells where there was a positive response, but it was very small (well below 1%).

Genuine participation

'They treat us like we're mushrooms. They keep us in the dark and feed us horse manure.'

Life on a low income means one is less able to fully participate in society. Whether such participation is manifest in education or leisure, political participation or having a voice in local/national decision making, it is a funda-

Table 5.8:

Aspects of local environment in the 15% most deprived areas and the rest of Scotland, Scotland, April 2004

	15% most deprived areas	Rest of Scotland	Scotland
	%	%	%
Population in proximity to EPER site, 2001			
Within 500m of a site	4.6	2.2	2.6
500 – 1000m	14.4	7.1	8.2
1000 – 2000m	28.3	19.3	20.7
More than 2,000m from a site	52.7	71.4	68.5
Within 500m of a derelict site, 2004	54.6	21.9	27.0
Selected aspects of neighbourhood that are particularly liked, 2003			
Quiet/peaceful	36	61	57
Nicely landscaped open spaces	9	20	18
Good neighbours	35	32	32
Good public transport	20	15	16
Like nothing about the area	12	3	4
Selected aspects of neighbourhood that are particularly disliked, 2003			
Young people hanging about/ nothing for young people to do	28	11	13
Vandalism	21	6	9
Drug abuse	18	4	6
Nowhere for children to play	9	4	5
Dislike nothing about the area	32	48	46

Source: Scottish Executive, *Social Focus on Deprived Areas 2005*, Scottish Executive, 2005, Tables 9.1, 9.3, 10.2 and 10.3

Note: The table presents area data, which will not coincide absolutely with low-income households (and households living in poverty). Furthermore, without specification of whether 15% equates with poverty, this data is only a measure of inequality, not poverty. Care has to be taken in interpreting this data when discussing poverty in Scotland.

mental right to which many people experiencing poverty have less experience of, and access to. As Table 5.9 shows, those living in households with lower incomes are also less likely to give up time to assist as a volunteer or organiser (for example, 16 per cent of those in households with an annual income of less than £6,000, compared with the Scottish average of 23 per cent).

Table 5.9:

Whether gave up time to help as a volunteer/organiser in the last 12 months by net annual household income, Scotland, 2003/04

	£0 – £6,000	£6,001 – £10,000	£10,001 – £15,000	£15,001 – £20,000	£20,001 – £25,000	£25,001 – £30,000	£30,001 – £40,000	Over £40,000	Scotland
	%	%	%	%	%	%	%	%	%
Gave up time as a volunteer/organiser in the last 12 months									
Yes	16	16	18	23	25	27	32	38	23
No	84	84	82	77	75	73	68	62	77
Base	2,465	5,486	5,814	4,023	3,121	2,495	2,724	1,557	27,649

Source: C Martin and others, *Scotland's People: Annual Report from the 2003/04 Scottish Household Survey*, Scottish Executive, 2005, Table 7.3

Note: See Table 5.1

Feeling powerless is an expression commonly used by people experiencing poverty. In order for people to feel they belong, they must feel their opinions matter and their voices must be heard in their local communities. Too frequently people feel ignored and unheard; the Get Heard project proved that people want to be heard and that they have an enormous amount of knowledge to give – if they are given the chance. Scottish society must tackle the sharing of power.

Conclusion

This chapter has demonstrated that poverty has far-ranging impacts on Scotland's poor. A lack of money directly leads to insecurity, debt, social exclusion and an inability to meet life's basic necessities. Poverty also strips people of their dignity and is associated with mental ill-health. Physical ill-health is more prevalent among the men, women, boys and girls of Scotland's poor. The lower life expectancies currently anticipated (and lower healthy life expectancy currently experienced) look set to continue as Scotland's poor live a less healthy lifestyle. Poorer communities are more likely to be less pleasant places to live, where concerns for personal safety are heightened. Finally, Scotland's poorest perceive themselves to be detached and disengaged from wider society.

Although a bleak picture has been portrayed of life on a low income in contemporary Scotland, sight must not be lost of the resilience of Scotland's poorest, aspects of quality in their lives and their desire to get on, get heard and overcome. The present need not determine the future if only we could find an effective means to support and enable Scotland's most vulnerable.

Notes:

1   JH McKendrick, K Backett-Milburn, SC Cunningham-Burley and G Scott, *Life in Low-income Families in Scotland: a review of the literature*, Scottish Executive, 2003; JH McKendrick, K Backett-Milburn and SC Cunningham-Burley, *Life in Low-income Families in Scotland*, Scottish Executive, 2003; B Holman, *Faith in the Poor*, Lion Publishing, 1998

2   L Burnett, *Dignity Shouldn't Have to be Earned*, The Poverty Alliance, 2006

3   The report was based on over 50 workshops involving 500 people across Scotland. Groups were self-selecting and were drawn mainly from the central belt of Scotland. The report acknowledges under-participation from those living in rural areas, from black and minority ethnic groups, from travellers' groups and from the low paid.

4   All five epigraphs are quotations drawn from people experiencing poverty, who participated in the Get Heard project.

5   JH McKendrick, K Backett-Milburn and SC Cunningham-Burley, *Life in Low-income Families in Scotland*, Scottish Executive Social Research, 2003

6   C Bromley and others, *Scottish Health Survey 2003*, Volume 2, Scottish Executive, 2005, Tables 1.4, 2.11, 3.4 and 4.7; C Bromley and others, *Scottish Health Survey 2003*, Volume 3, Scottish Executive, 2005, Tables 1.9, 2.7, 3.4 and 4.7

Section Three
Combating poverty

Six

Introduction: tackling poverty through the policy, practice and provision of services

Gerry Mooney

This section consists of a series of essays on different aspects of poverty. We have drawn together a range of contributions from anti-poverty campaigners, researchers, activists and academics who are involved in a diverse range of activities in relation to poverty or who undertake research on particular aspects of poverty. These are not designed to offer a full and detailed analysis; rather, the authors provide an overview of the key issues affecting their particular area of practice, knowledge or expertise.

Whatever the approach and opinions taken by authors – and readers will discover considerable diversity across these contributions – all have been tasked to summarise the key policy measures in their field, consider their effectiveness and or limitations, and also to generate any recommendations for a more useful approach to tackling the problems of poverty. While there is diversity, there is also some shared thinking across the different chapters. In particular, key areas of UK government policy, notably welfare to work, are regarded as being only partially effective in tackling poverty, while for some, the key objective of UK government policy is less with offering an effective means of addressing poverty, and more about disciplining and punishing those who are reluctant to enter low-paid and poor-quality work.

In any collection such as this it is difficult to provide comprehensive coverage of all areas of poverty and social exclusion. The areas included here for discussion were not chosen on the grounds that these are more important than other areas of poverty, but more that they illuminate poverty in general – while in other cases, for instance with regard to minority ethnic groups, childless adults and rural poverty, to highlight areas that have often been neglected and/or marginalised in the discussion of poverty. Bearing in mind that this is being produced in the months running up to the 2007 Scottish elections, it is hoped that these neglected areas are helped to a more prominent position in debates.

While each of the essays considers a particular aspect of poverty, clearly there is a wider recognition that these topics and issues are inter-related in a wide range of both direct and indirect ways. Issues of family poverty (Chapter 12), taking one case study for example, are related to the provision of quality, affordable childcare (Chapter 16) and so on.

As might be expected, particular issues are featured prominently in this section, for example, active labour market policy and financial exclusion. As we saw in Chapter 4, poverty is not evenly distributed throughout the population but tends to affect particular groups of people and, therefore, we have opted to include contributions that focus on specific groups, for instance asylum seekers, families and childless adults. Where one lives (places) often has a major influence on both susceptibility to poverty and on how poverty is experienced. Issues, people and places overlap throughout.

Taken together, these short essays reflect the sub-title of this section – combating poverty through policy, practice and the provision (and delivery) of services. Depending on the issue at hand, the balance between policy, practice and provision will differ, and that they often overlap in any case means that any 'separation' is artificial. However, there is another rationale to this structure: a key argument in this book is that in addition to policies, practice and delivery of public services have important roles to play in combating poverty. Adequate policies and strategies are, of course, a necessity but all too often the actual application of policy, here referred to as the practice of policy, is frequently neglected. As is being increasingly recognised by our governments, particularly at local level, the co-ordination of service planning and delivery can be important adjuncts to other areas of poverty policy. Failure to plan effectively, coupled with a policy practice that is harsh and even punitive, can only work to reinforce stigmatisation while further exacerbating problems of social exclusion.

In Section Four we revisit some of the main themes of Section Three and draw out some important conclusions for the direction of anti-poverty policy in Scotland in the immediate future. We now turn to highlight some of the main issues that feature in debates and arguments over poverty in Scotland today.

Seven
Financial inclusion
Morag Gillespie

As the UK government and Scottish Parliament grapple with targets on reducing poverty, levels of personal debt and consumer credit amongst all income groups are rising sharply across the UK.[1] Indebtedness is now a key policy concern, there is growing recognition that affordable credit or borrowing is not equally accessible across the population, and many people do not have the most basic of financial products.

> There is a large minority of people for whom the financial services revolution has effectively passed them by.[2]

People living in poverty are most likely to lack such products or services and a significant minority of people in the UK do not use or have access to insurance, savings and investments, mainstream credit, and bank or building society accounts.[3] Around one in twelve people in the UK do not have bank accounts, but Citizens Advice Scotland estimates that the figure is higher in Scotland at 12 per cent.[4] This chapter provides a summary of some key recent financial inclusion policy initiatives affecting Scotland and considers the specific issue of access to bank accounts.

Policy responses to financial exclusion

Financial inclusion and 'asset-based welfare' are increasingly being promoted as sustainable routes to reducing and preventing poverty and social exclusion. These complement approaches that aim to increase incomes by encouraging savings, promoting bank accounts and providing financial education.[5] The UK government identifies promotion of financial inclusion as crucial to overcoming poverty. Towards the aim of increasing assets and reducing financial exclusion, it is: providing support for increased access to money advice; working towards a 'shared goal' with the banking industry to reduce by half the number of adults with no bank account;[6] promoting savings through the Child Trust Fund; providing an additional £210 million for the social fund budgetary loan scheme over the next three years; and administering a growth fund, which supports credit unions and other third-sector lenders. The Department for Work and Pensions argues that such measures are essential to ensure:

> ... long-term independence and financial inclusion, and for breaking intergenerational poverty... and wil increase the availability of affordable credit to low-income families.[7]

The Scottish Executive produced a financial inclusion action plan in 2005 as a key element of *Closing the Opportunity Gap*, its strategy to tackle poverty. It aims '... to improve financial inclusion for vulnerable groups of people and communities at key transition points in people's lives'.[8] The Scottish Executive defines financial inclusion as:

> ... access for individuals to appropriate financial products and services. This includes people having the skills, knowledge and understanding to make best use of those products and services.

The action plan outlines a similar approach to that of the UK government. It acknowledges that low-income groups are less likely to have a bank or building society account or insurance, and are more likely to be in arrears with consumer credit or household bills. As part of the overall objective of reducing the vulnerability of low-income families to over-indebtedness and to lift them out of poverty, the target set is:

> ... by 2008, to increase the availability of appropriate financial services and money advice to low-income families to reduce their vulnerability to financial exclusion and multiple debts.[9]

A range of projects and activities is being put in place to address: financial education; access to affordable budgeting and repayment methods, and to savings, pensions and information to prevent financial exclusion; protection from loan sharks; and access to affordable credit, mainstream banking services and home contents insurance. Measures include support for money advice services, credit unions and community banking; exploring alternative approaches to fair credit, and community and social housing-based insurance schemes; and operating a mortgage-to-rent scheme.

Legislative changes in Scotland have included replacing poinding and warrant sales with a national debt arrangements scheme to implement the Debt Arrangement and Attachment (Scotland) Act 2002. There is a strong focus on money advice, with funding for both frontline service provision and action research to find routes to improving access to such advice, quality standards, and training linked to the introduction of the debt arrangements scheme. Added to other Scottish initiatives (such as support for setting up and developing credit unions) and joint initiatives with the UK government, these developments represent considerable sustained effort to address financial exclusion in Scotland.

Making a difference?

Although it has been helpful to quantify the problems associated with financial exclusion, Bremner believes there has been 'a conspicuous lack of solutions, in the form of actual products' to meet the needs of those who are financially excluded.[10] In Scotland, the new debt arrangements scheme is an example of the problem. Few people mourn poinding and warrant sales, but rights and advice workers are expressing disappointment that the new scheme is not helping many people on low incomes – put simply, unless people have some available income or assets to arrange debt repayments, the current scheme has no relevance for them.[11]

Many of the projects and initiatives that are being undertaken have yet to bear fruit. However, Bremner highlights missed opportunities such as regulating credit providers more directly in the new Consumer Credit Act; she views as problematic the Government's reliance on the finance industry for solutions and the policy emphasis on empowering customers rather than generating the products they need.[12]

For example, having a bank account is viewed by the Government as a key indicator of financial inclusion. The drive to pay benefits through bank accounts has contributed to reducing the number of people without accounts. However, many people opened post office card accounts and not bank accounts. These have helped people who cannot provide the forms of identification required for a bank account. However, although included as part of the Government's initial drive to encourage use of bank accounts, post office card accounts look set to disappear in 2010 when they will no longer be acceptable for direct payment of benefits.

This prospect raises concerns for disadvantaged groups. Not all basic and current accounts allow holders to access their money at a post office counter – at present a particularly important issue for Scotland's rural communities where bank branches are disappearing.[13] Citizens Advice highlighted that, of cash machines available, 43 per cent now charge a fee and that flat fees hit hardest those who make small withdrawals. Furthermore, an Edinburgh CAB highlighted that in some urban areas people face a 30-minute walk for a free machine.[14] Benefits payments into bank accounts can disappear through fees charged for withdrawing funds or failed direct debits.[15] Some people have been encouraged towards inappropriate accounts and services, and particular concerns remain about the treatment of people with learning difficulties.[16]

Time is short to address a host of problems around accessible banking. The Post Office may develop an alternative account, credit unions may develop accounts that are acceptable for benefit payments, more bank accounts may become available at post offices and the trend in fee-charging cash machines may reverse. These things are possible, but unlikely to happen in the systematic way and at the pace required to protect disadvantaged groups who remain at risk of inappropriate accounts, borrowing, services and costs, and ongoing problems with accessing benefits. Substituting the high interest rates charged by doorstep lenders with bank charges does not represent the sort of progress that is needed.

At present, having a bank account is not a measure of financial inclusion and may even exacerbate the financial difficulties encountered by people experiencing poverty. As a minimum the Government must guarantee access to benefits without incurring costs. Unless the barriers to such a guarantee can be addressed quickly, it must rethink its approach to paying benefits.

Finally, financial inclusion measures do not substitute for addressing income poverty. People on low incomes have to be good at managing their money and the Government should not be making that task harder. Financial inclusion will have much more meaning for people when the products they need are available and they have sufficient income to make choices.

Notes

1   C Sharp, *On the Cards: the debt crisis facing Scottish CAB clients*, Citizens Advice Scotland, 2004; E Kempson, S McKay and M Willits, *Characteristics of*

Families in Debt and the Nature of Indebtedness, DWP Research Report No. 211, Corporate Document Services, 2004

2 F Reynolds, 'Promoting Financial Inclusion', *Poverty* 114, CPAG, 2003

3 See note 2

4 D McNeish, *Post Office Card Accounts*, Briefing For Members Debate, 30 March 2006

5 See note 2

6 Department for Work and Pensions, *Opportunity for All: seventh annual report*, The Stationery Office, 2005, p38

7 Department for Work and Pensions, *Making a Difference: tackling poverty – a progress report*, The Stationery Office, 2006, p11

8 Scottish Executive, *Financial Inclusion Action Plan*, 2005, p4

9 See note 8, p6

10 A Bremner, 'Financial Exclusion and Poverty', *The Poverty Report Card 2005*, The Poverty Alliance, 2005, p21

11 G Blount, 'Ghosts of Christmas Past: the poor pay more', *Scottish Anti-poverty Review*, Vol 2, Winter 2005, pp14-16

12 See note 10

13 House of Commons, *Hansard* Written Answers, 2006, col 1955w

14 Citizens Advice, *Cash Machine Charges: fifth report from the Treasury Committee and the Government's response*, 2006; Citizens Advice Scotland, Bank Charges, Briefing Paper 20, Citizens Advice Scotland, 2006

15 See note 14

16 M Hurcombe, *Banking on Change: increased access to banking services by people with learning disabilities*, Edinburgh Voluntary Sector Forum for Services to People with Learning Disabilities and FAIR Ltd, 2004

Eight

Tackling income poverty through local taxation

Christine Cooper, Mike Danson and Geoff Whittam

The potential of local taxation to tackle income poverty has been the sub-ject of recent debate. Various options promoted by political parties in Scotland include reform of the council tax or replacement with a local income or land tax.[1] We contribute to the debate by focusing on one par-ticular approach – a Scottish service tax. We explain how the tax system has increased income inequality. We argue that one of the main causes of income poverty over the last two decades is the increasingly regressive nature of the taxation system. One of the most regressive forms of taxa-tion is council tax and in this chapter we argue that this needs to be scrapped and replaced with a Scottish service tax (SST),[2] a progressive local income tax. Whilst not fully eliminating income poverty, it will certainly reduce levels of income poverty by redistributing income from the rich to the poor and exempting those on the lowest incomes from payment alto-gether. We explain how SST would operate, and finally look at the impact of the SST for the economy as a whole and for certain occupational groups.

Background

The move in the 1980s away from progressive direct taxation to regres-sive indirect taxation has led to people on the lowest incomes paying a greater proportion of their income in tax than those on the highest levels of income. Thus, while the poorest fifth had one-quarter of their income taxed in 1983 (27 per cent), this had *risen* to two-fifths of their income by 1999 (41 per cent). On the other hand, the richest fifth had two-fifths of their income taxed in 1983 (41 per cent), only for this to *fall* to one-third of their income by 1999 (35 per cent).

It is useful to recall that in 1987/88, even after almost nine years of the Thatcher Government, the highest rate of income tax was 60 per cent, with a progression in five percentage point steps from 40 per cent beyond the basic rate of 27 per cent. Since then, there have effectively been but two rates, now 23 per cent and 40 per cent.

At the local level, the regressive nature of the current council tax makes the problem even worse. Under the former rating system the ratio of the highest to the lowest rates payable was 14:1; under the council tax it is 3:1. The large numbers who rely on the means-tested council tax benefit in Scotland (590,000) are testament to the regressive nature of this tax. To address these needs, and to improve the nature of the tax system, requires an innovative approach. A progressive local income tax can be justified on the grounds of equity and the other characteristics of what makes a good tax (as classically defined by Adam Smith). Plus, through a more just distribution formula to apportion the rate support grant between Scottish local authorities, it will free up resources to be delivered locally for the benefit of the socially excluded.

The Scottish service tax

An SST should be established at the Scottish level, with revenues distributed across local government areas according to needs. Such a national tax would avoid the problems of fiscal flight, where those who could afford it move their residential location to suburban commuting areas with fewer social difficulties and less poverty, allowing lower tax rates to be set, while the cities and depressed poor communities have to impose ever higher tax rates. The failure of other models – including 'local' models – of local income taxes to recognise this point is not insubstantial in the fight against poverty, as an ill-conceived local income tax regime could exacerbate, rather than address, poverty in Scotland. In this context and the terms of the Scotland Act,[3] the SST also should be dedicated to local government expenditure and, with the recognition of the advantages of holistic policy implementation, the expansion of budgets, particularly in Scotland's poorer areas, should lead to significant improvements in the health, education and housing conditions of Scotland's citizens. This redistribution from the rich to the poor should also lead to an expansion of the Scottish economy.[4]

The report on local government finance by the Layfield Committee identified problems with a local income tax, although considered it to be a 'serious candidate' for financing local authority expenditure.[5] We believe that the SST overcomes the problems identified by Layfield: namely costs, fiscal flight and UK demand management.[6] Additionally, the Scottish Parliament has the authority and legitimacy under the Scotland Act to alter the form of taxation for local authority spending, as long as the proceeds are used to fund local authority expenditure.[7]

It is proposed that non-domestic tax policy and business rate levels should be returned to local authority control. This has been supported by the Local Government Committee of the Scottish Executive.[8] By suggesting that the business rate would be set, collected and retained locally, the loss of direct control over their revenues raised from domestic residents would be offset by the autonomy that would accompany the return of this tax power. Local authorities already bill and collect non-domestic rates

Table 8.1:
Levels of tax in the Scottish service tax model, 2002/03

Range of total income (lower limit)	Total number liable for tax	Total income tax paid	Marginal rate	Total SST paid	Average SST paid	Average income	SST paid as % of income
£	000s	£m	%	£000	£	£	%
4,615	38	1	0.0	0	0	4,842	0.0
5,000	614	219	0.0	0	0	7,606	0.0
10,000	580	740	4.5	63,000	109	12,414	0.9
15,000	428	973	4.5	141,300	330	17,336	1.9
20,000	490	1,808	4.5	315,450	644	24,306	2.6
30,000	178	1,040	15.0	275,700	1,549	34,326	4.5
40,000	43	371	15.0	119,700	2,784	42,558	6.5
45,000	28	292	15.0	97,200	3,471	47,143	7.4
50,000	53	765	18.0	282,300	5,326	57,925	9.2
70,000	18	400	18.0	163,800	9,100	78,889	11.5
90,000	21	1,150	20.0	563,100	26,814	168,571	15.9
Total	2,491	7,759		2,021,550	812	19,540	4.2

Source: Authors' own estimates

Note: Compared with the anticipated council tax (including council tax benefit) collected over that period (£1.753 billion) this represents an increase of about £269 million.

and this return of control, therefore, creates no problems in relation to the mechanisms required.

Winners and losers

Table 8.1 illustrates the revenue generation potential had the SST been deployed in 2002/03 in place of council tax. It shows that even if Westminster insists on retaining the approximate £300 million paid in council tax benefit, the SST would have raised £269 million more than council tax.

The introduction of a fairer tax system comes at a price; there are winners and losers. For example, those earning £70,000 a year would pay (on 2002/03 calculations) around £9,100 in SST, while those earning less than £15,000 a year would pay around £330. These figures are, respectively, far in excess and far below the equivalent current council tax charges for an individual. We would argue that increased taxation for the rich is a price worth paying with regard to the nation as a whole: greater equity leads to economic growth within the economy and enhances greater opportunities for the poor, with the increased taxation spent on welfare and education provision, for example, to develop skills to ensure that this growth becomes sustainable.[9]

In conclusion, the SST is based on sound economic research, it meets the criteria of a 'good tax', and will lead to benefits for the poorest in our community, without fundamentally damaging the macroeconomic environment. All models of a reformed council tax would still leave a tax which is not progressive, is not based on ability to pay and, to offer some protection, relies on council tax benefit, which is notoriously complex to claim and has low rates of take-up. An SST will directly impact on poverty and the causes of poverty by raising the disposable incomes of the poorest in society without means-testing, and indirectly by generating economic expansion and allowing greater investment in public services.

Notes

1   See for example, *Scottish Labour Manifesto*, 2003, available online at www.scottishlabour.org.uk/manifestosection26; *Scottish Liberal Democrat Election Manifesto*, 2005, available online at www.scottishlibdems.org.uk/the party.ge2005/supplement.shtm/#council%20tax; SNP Policy Unit Saltire Paper

2/04, available online at www.snp.org/policies/government-communities/copy ofindex_html/2006-08.1256400194/download; Green Party Press Release, 12 March 2004, available online at www.scottishgreens.org.uk/site/id/4133

2   M Danson and G Whittam, 'The Case for a Scottish Service Tax', *Capital and Class*, Vol 81, 2003, pp61–83

3   D Heald and A McLeod, *The Laws of Scotland: Stair Memorial Encyclopaedia*, Butterworths, 2002

4   P McGregor, J Stevens, K Swales and YP Yin, 'Some Simple Macro-economics of Scottish Devolution', in M Danson, S Hill and G Lloyd (eds), *Regional Governance and Economic Development: European research in regional science 7*, Pion, 1997, pp187–209; I McNicoll, 'A New Approach to Modelling the Scottish Economy', *Mimeo*, Scottish Enterprise, 2003

5   Layfield Committee, *Report of the Committee of Enquiry into Local Government Finance*, HMSO, 1976

6   T Jackson, 'Tax Varying Powers: the watchdog that will not bark', in J McCarthy and D Newlands (eds), *Governing Scotland: problems and prospects*, Ashgate, 1999, pp69–85; see also note 2, p462

7   The Scotland Act 1998

8   Local Government Committee *Report on Inquiry into Local Government Finance, Volume 1*, 6th Report, 2002, recommendation xii: 'Accordingly, the Committee recommends the Scottish Executive to introduce legislation to return the non-domestic rate to local control at the earliest opportunity'.

9   World Bank, *World Development Report*, Oxford University Press, 2006

Nine

Poverty and employability: a problem drug use perspective

David Liddell

Introduction

Employability has moved up the anti-poverty agenda in recent years. Although it is a term that is widely used, 'employability' can mean a variety of things in different contexts. In the Scottish Executive's recently published employability framework, *Workforce Plus*, it is defined as '... the combination of factors and processes which enable people to progress towards or get into employment, to stay in employment and to move on in the workplace'.[1] To improve employability is, therefore, to address the barriers that people face in returning to the labour market, both individual and institutional, and to ensure that they have the correct support to stay there. Given the wide range of barriers that people can encounter, the type of policy interventions potentially covered by employability strategies is very broad indeed. In this chapter, we focus on the relationship between problem drug use, employability and poverty.

Changing policy

Drug policy has changed markedly over the last twenty years, although all approaches have acknowledged the close association between problem drug use and multiple deprivation.[2] It is fairly self-evident, therefore, that we must respond to causal factors, rather than focusing solely on 'treating the symptoms', if we are to reduce drug problems and the number of problem drug users. The significance of problem drug use has also been acknowledged when focusing on the problems faced by populations at risk of poverty and deprivation – for example, offenders going into and leaving prison.[3] Reflection on drug policy since the early 1980s – when drug problems rose dramatically n Scotland – will furnish us with a better understanding of how the links between drugs policy and employment, skills and employability policy in Scotland have developed.

An increase in heroin use was observed in the early 1980s particularly around the housing schemes of Glasgow, Edinburgh and Dundee. In 1984, the (then) Scottish Office funded small community-based initiatives recognising that the problems stemmed from deprivation, high unemployment and 'poverty of aspiration'. This was followed by significantly more emphasis on a criminal justice response, which attempted to stem the supply routes and resulted in the incarceration of large numbers of heroin users.

Public health concerns came to drive drug policy following the identification in 1985 of high levels of HIV.[4] As HIV concerns dominated, social factors (for example, poor housing, unemployment and debt) receded in terms of influencing the policy agenda. Prior to HIV health treatment, services for problem drug users had taken a back seat, but now were at the forefront of the response. Additional funding was also forthcoming to establish needle exchanges and prescribing services.

The 1990s saw a consolidation and expansion of these services and the first drug strategy for Scotland was published in 1994, which began to highlight the need for more holistic services.[5] The 1999 report by the Scottish Parliament's Social Inclusion Committee into *Drug Misuse and Deprived Communities* reinforced this perspective.[6]

The first term of the Scottish Parliament focused heavily on social inclusion and an early development of the Scottish Executive was the creation of the New Futures funding initiative. This was developed by Scottish Enterprise with the support of Wendy Alexander. Alexander championed the approach with First Minister Donald Dewar when she was a political adviser, and then as the Scottish Executive's first Enterprise Minister. The initiative recognised that for most vulnerable adults, the transition to work would not be straightforward, that being in meaningful employment was far from the current situation of most of this group, and there would be many hurdles to overcome.

Scottish Enterprise initially held discussions with frontline agencies who were working with a range of the most vulnerable adults including those with mental health problems, histories of offending and experience of homelessness, as well as drug users. The conclusion was that it was crucial to take employability provision to clients. That meant putting provision into frontline care services rather than waiting for people to be referred on to employability programmes, having first progressed, perhaps after many years, through the treatment and care sector. This approach recognised the social and environmental factors which impact on the development of a person's drug problem, homelessness or offending, and that a key factor in assisting people to overcome these problems is to give them hope that there is an alternative to their current situation and a better life beyond their immediate problems.

New Futures was small-scale but was judged by Scottish Enterprise to have made a substantial impact. The phase 2 outcomes (2002 to 2005) built on the success of the earlier phase to deliver:

- 21 per cent into employment or self-employment;
- 12 per cent into further education and community education;
- 14 per cent into government programmes;
- 10 per cent into voluntary work.[7]

However, projects often failed to secure mainstream funding on the grounds that the outcomes were inadequate. In general terms, this meant that insufficient numbers achieving hard outcomes like jobs. The softer outcomes of the initiative were considered by funders to be too woolly and not giving sufficient value for money. This led to considerable uncertainty about continued funding of New Futures, but following a Parliamentary motion signed by a majority of MSPs, the Executive gave a further year's funding in 2005/06. A further two years' funding (£3.1m) for 2006–2008 has now been put into the community planning partnerships for 'New Futures-type provision'.

2002 heralded the launch of the Jobcentre Plus initiative, *Progress2Work* (P2W), which specifically targeted problem drug users. New Futures and P2W were complementary in that New Futures worked with those a significant way from the labour market, who could then move on to the more job-focused P2W.

In January 2006, the Department for Work and Pensions launched its Green Paper, *A New Deal For Welfare: empowering people to work*. This makes numerous references to results-based outcomes, with its language couched in terms of hard indicators of success – not an encouraging sign for those working with the most marginalised client groups furthest from the labour market. At the same time, Scottish Enterprise has moved away from 'social inclusion' to concentrate on 'enterprise' with the New Futures-type of provision moving to community planning partnerships. However, most treatment and care services are still not engaging effectively with this agenda.

Where next?

The difficulty when looking at poverty and employability in relation to problematic drug use is that we still view drug dependency as either a disease which needs curing or a deviant criminal activity from which society needs to be protected. These analyses fail to acknowledge that social factors of poverty and deprivation (self-esteem and self-worth) play a significant part in creating and perpetuating drug problems.

A greater acknowledgement of this would result in a fundamental re-think of our services, so that early employability – with clear and encouraging signage of routes out for drug users – becomes an integral part of frontline services for all who could benefit from it, rather than being an after-thought.

The Scottish Executive's *Moving On* report highlighted the difficulty of assessing those who could benefit from employability programmes, and it seems sensible to wider focus to early employability (for example, literacy and numeracy skills).[8] We must get into a position where the outcomes are dictated by the individual, rather than the funders of the service. This is needs-led services in the wider sense and will involve developing new ways of commissioning services which cut through the treatment/welfare and employability divide.

But the danger remains that early employability programmes for drug users and other groups facing the biggest barriers to engaging with work will not have hard enough outcomes for funders to buy into this agenda. Success should be measured in terms of 'soft' as well as 'hard' outcomes – such as evaluating the journey along the path, rather than just whether someone secured a job at the end of a specific period of time. Furthermore, the political argument – that investment at an earlier stage will deliver hard outcomes (employment) further down the line – needs to be pressed, and won, continually, if those furthest from the labour market are to benefit from a policy focus that sees work as the key route out of poverty.

Notes

1   Scottish Executive, *Workforce Plus: an employability framework for Scotland*, 2006

2   The Scottish Office, *Tackling Drugs in Scotland*, The Stationery Office, 1999

3   R Houchin, *Social Exclusion and Imprisonment In Scotland*, Glasgow Caledonian University, 2005

4   Department of Health and Social Security, *AIDS and Drug Misuse Part 1*, Report by the Advisory Council on the Misuse of Drugs, HMSO, 1988

5   The Scottish Office Home and Health Department, *Drugs in Scotland: meeting the challenge*, HMSO, 1994

6   Scottish Parliament, Social Inclusion, Housing and Voluntary Sector Committee, *Inquiry into Drug Misuse and Deprived Communities*, Sixth report, The Stationery Office, 2000

7   Scottish Enterprise, *Evaluations of New Futures*, Phase 1 and 2, 2005

8   Scottish Executive Effective Interventions Unit, *Moving On: education, training and employment for recovering drug users*, 2001

Ten

Poverty and health

Janet Muir and Elspeth Gracey

> Although it has been proven that many low-income families do try to improve
> the diet of their children by buying wholemeal bread, fresh fruit, vegetables
> and pasta, the high cost of trying to feed your family day by day makes it
> impossible not to buy the more filling high fat and sugar-laden foods. To
> wander around a glossy supermarket with very little money in your purse, it's
> little wonder that this leads to depression, a sense of never coping and
> always having to make a choice between heating your home or buying a
> wholesome varied diet for your family. It's a constant battle, leading to low
> self-esteem and a feeling of helplessness and despair.[1]

This chapter explores the impact of poverty on health. It draws on the
knowledge, expertise and experience of community health organisations
operating in Scotland's low-income communities, together with the
insights of community development practitioners within the Community
Health Exchange, and argues that community development is an essential approach to tackling poverty and inequalities at the local level.

Poverty and health inequalities

Poverty can lead to ill-health, and ill-health can contribute to keeping people poor. The associations and inter-relationships between poverty and
health have been researched extensively. Indeed, since the Black Report
in early 1980s,[2] many studies in Britain have described how the gap in
healthy living and life expectancy between people living in poverty and
those living in prosperity has widened.[3]

There are stark contrasts between the poorest 10 per cent of
Britain's population who are in receipt of 3 per cent of the total income,
and the wealthiest 10 per cent who are in receipt of more than a quarter
of the total income.[4] The poverty gap in life expectancy between those liv-

ing in Britain's least healthy area (Glasgow) and the healthiest area (East Dorset) is 11 years for men and 8.4 years for women.

The effects of poverty on health inequalities are even more staggering in Scotland's largest city. For example, in Glasgow at a small-area level (for example, postcode sectors), differences in life expectancy can be up to 25 years for men and 15 years for women.[5] If we examine the quality of life, health determinants, and life choices, the scale of the challenge for policy makers becomes apparent.

Closing the health gap: what to prioritise?

A range of approaches have been adopted in policy and practice to tackle poverty and health inequalities; some are aimed at generating more inclusive services, some at changing individual behaviour, and some at the redistribution of wealth and resources. The current Labour Government has primarily advocated that the route from poverty is through gainful employment. Many institutions, voluntary organisations and campaigns have called for more radical fiscal policies beyond a focus on welfare to work. For example, the Townsend Centre for International Poverty Research advocated:[6]

- increased welfare benefits and pensions;
- a reduction in means-testing;
- increases in universal benefits, such as child benefit;
- greater provision of affordable social housing;
- removal of standing charges for utilities and the outlawing of differential pricing structures which result in the poorest paying most for essential good and services;
- annual increase in the national minimum wage at a rate greater than the rise in average wages.

However, governments, academics and practitioners have reached a broad consensus that partnership working is required between agencies and with communities if we are to significantly impact on poverty and reduce health inequalities. The belief is that agencies working together with communities will be in a stronger position to tackle the inter-related challenges of poverty and health inequalities.[7]

Scotland has embraced partnership working at a local level. The implementation of community planning partnerships (see Chapter 17) and community health partnerships has redesigned service delivery in health and social regeneration to harness the anticipated added value of inter-agency working, public participation and community engagement. Partnership working at the local level presents an opportunity for people living in poverty to make decision making more responsive to their needs. Furthermore, involvement leads to the acquisition of experience and skills, which may lead to routes out of poverty.[8]

The Scottish Executive's health improvement and social policies also promote a mixture of other 'local' solutions. Principally through *Improving Scotland's Health: the challenge* and *Closing the Opportunity Gap*, resources are targeted at low-income areas by promoting mental health and well-being, community regeneration, social integration, and individual behavioural change – focusing on stopping smoking, increasing physical activity, promoting positive sexual health and a healthy diet.[9] In relation to health care, the Minister for Health launched *Delivering for Health*, a new framework for the NHS to 'tackle the causes of ill-health' and provide 'care which is quicker, more personal and closer to home'.[10]

The role and impact of community-led health

Community development involves:

- promoting learning, knowledge, skills, confidence and the capacity to act collectively;
- taking positive action to address inequalities in power, access and participation;
- strengthening organisation, networking and leadership with and between communities;
- working for change through increased local democracy, participation and involvement in public affairs.

Taken together, the evidence shows that these four processes can lead to communities having greater control and influence on positive health, social, economic and environmental outcomes, which result in a better quality of life for all people.

Community health initiatives within the Community Health Exchange have adopted these processes and have had significant success in addressing poverty and tackling health inequalities.[11] Three examples are presented in Table 10.1; each initiative operates in an impoverished area and is grounded in a social model of health.

Table 10.1:

Local action on poverty and health inequality: Community Health Exchange in practice

Initiating opportunities for people with mental health problems to earn 'local currency' in a local exchange trading scheme (LETS) in Stirling. **Let's Make it Better** reported improved self-esteem, opportunities to participate on equal terms within the local community, opportunity to access services, control over level of participation and developing more productive ways of working with health professionals.

Supporting South Asian women in Edinburgh to undertake participatory research into their health needs. **Nari Kallyan Shangho Community Health Project** reported reduced reliance on anti-depressants, reduced isolation, enhanced social networks, access to appropriate childcare facilities and improved communication between service providers and South Asian women.

Establishing new services such as a stress centre and home safety project in the east end of Glasgow. **The East End Health Action Community Health Project** reported an increase in health awareness, integration of community development approaches into mainstream services and more locally relevant policies and practice.

The challenge ahead

Tackling the root causes of poverty requires more radical steps than community development alone. Furthermore, focusing only on specific geographic areas will fail to address the needs of the substantial proportion of poor people who do not live in poor areas. However, community development has an important role to play in overcoming poverty and the impact on health; in the absence of structural change at the macro level, more significant impact through community health development will be impeded.

Crucially, the success of the community development approach should be gauged on how small initiatives are translated into effective strategic approaches across the country, which impact on poverty and health inequalities in localities of need. Lessons derived from these case studies demonstrate the essential elements of good practice – that is, they:

- promote empowerment of individuals and collectives;
- promote social justice and challenge inequalities;
- enable and support community members to take 'ownership' of their health improvement, and to identify and take action on their health priorities;
- embrace group work, participatory appraisal, and 'planning for real', approaches which support people to effect change in systems that affect their lives;
- support community members to develop confidence, skills and self-esteem;
- embed equalities, supporting the inclusion and participation of the most excluded individuals and groups;
- develop and implement policies which tackle barriers to participation – for example, use of language and use of appropriate venues;
- enable community members to challenge and work with established power bases in the community, public and voluntary sector;
- encourage inter-agency working with community organisations and networking;
- embrace evaluation to demonstrate health and social impacts resulting from resource deployment and action.

Embedding these approaches in health improvement structures and service delivery is a significant challenge. Those more familiar with the medical model of health improvement, and less aware of the intrinsic health-improving capacity of community development will be sceptical. Thus, calls for more research to demonstrate the health benefits of community development and community-led health are to be welcomed. Most welcome of all, however is the strategic approach to implementation, which is currently being assisted through the work of the National Task Group, *Community-Led: supporting and developing healthy communities*.[12] We all need greater recognition of, and more opportunities for, community development approaches to tackling poverty and health inequalities.

Notes

1   NHS Health Scotland, *Writing About Health Issues: voices from communities*, 2004

2   Department of Health and Social Security, *Inequalities in Health: report of a research working group*, 1980

3   For example, R Wilkinson, *Impact of Health Inequalities*, Routledge, 2005

4   M Shaw, G Davey Smith and D Dorling, 'Health Inequalities and New Labour: how the promises compare with real progress', *British Medical Journal*, 2005, Vol 330, pp1016–21

5   NHS Health Scotland, *Community Health Profiles*, 2005

6   See Townsend Centre for International Poverty Research, available at: http://www.bris.ac.uk/poverty/index.html

7   C Huxham and S Vangen, *Managing to Collaborate: the theory and practice of collaborative advantage*, Routledge, 2005

8   NHS Health Scotland, *Health Issues in the Community*, 2002; J Jones, *Private Troubles and Public Issues*, 2002; A Kennedy and J Cosgrove, *Insight: case studies in community development and health in Scotland*, 2003

9   Scottish Executive, *Improving Scotland's Health: the Challenge*, 2003; Scottish Executive, *Closing the Opportunity Gap*, 2003

10   Scottish Executive, *Delivering for Health*, 2005

11   See Community Health Exchange, available at: www.chex.org.uk

12   NHS Health Scotland, *Community-Led: supporting and developing healthy communities*, Briefing Paper, March 2006

Eleven

Child poverty

John Dickie

Introduction

Child poverty in Scotland, as in the rest of the UK, remains extremely high. In recent historical terms, in relation to other European countries, and compared to adults, children in Scotland face an unusually high risk of poverty. Nearly one in four children are officially recognised as poor, compared with 18 per cent of the population as a whole, and there are twice as many children now living in poverty as there were in 1979.[1] Moreover, Scotland's children are more than twice as likely to be poor than their peers in neighbouring Scandinavian countries.[2]

Whilst child poverty remains high, the number of children in poverty has been decreasing, markedly so since this volume was last published in 2002. Unprecedented government commitments to eradicate child poverty within a generation, and policy action from both Westminster and Holyrood to support those commitments, are having an impact – providing an important lesson for anti-poverty ambitions generally, that, with political will and investment, policy can reduce poverty.

Yet thousands of our children continue to miss out on the basics: on adequate clothes and shoes, on healthy food, on educational opportunities and on the social activities that bind children to their families, friends and wider communities. Poverty continues to grind down the quality of children's lives and stunt their life chances.

This chapter explains how policy has worked to reduce child poverty, outlines why progress has only gone so far, and indicates the action needed to ensure the vision of a Scotland free of child poverty by 2020 is realised.

Recent child poverty policy

Since 2002 three key principles have underpinned child poverty policy within central and devolved government. First, paid work is viewed as the key route out of poverty; second, targeting is seen as the most effective way of providing additional support to families; and third, there has been an underlying assumption that eradicating child poverty is possible without challenging underlying income inequalities.

Increasing the numbers of parents in work is at the heart of central and devolved government strategy to end child poverty. At UK level, policy has focused on increasing the numbers of people in work by promoting economic growth, the New Deals and reforming the benefits system. Rights to benefits have increasingly been accompanied by support to engage with employment, but also a stress on responsibilities, accompanied by compulsion and threat of benefit sanctions.

Government has taken action to make work pay by introducing the national minimum wage and increasing in-work support through working tax credit. Financial support to families, both in and out of work, has also been increased through child tax credit.

Increasing employment is also the first of the six objectives in the Scottish Executive's *Closing the Opportunity Gap* strategy to tackle poverty.[3] Specific work-focused child poverty policy initiatives include the Working for Families fund, targeting resources on twenty local authorities to help parents, particularly lone parents, toward employment by overcoming childcare problems.

Closing the Opportunity Gap has been welcomed for recognising the need for a 'joined-up' approach and for demanding the full range of Executive departments contribute to tackling poverty. In relation to child poverty specifically, targets reflect the belief that income-related child poverty policy needs to be complemented by policies to improve opportunities for some of Scotland's most excluded children. Policy ambitions to increase the attainment levels of the lowest-performing 20 per cent of pupils and to ensure that children facing particular disadvantage have an '... integrated package of appropriate health, care and education support', are included in the ten targets, as is support for children leaving local authority care.[4] A further strand in devolved policy has been the *Hungry for Success* programme, seeking to improve nutrition and take-up of school meals as part of a wider health inequalities agenda.[5] There has, however, been no use of the Scottish Parliament's power to vary the basic rate of income tax or to reform local taxation (Chapter 8).

Child poverty policy: a brief critique

The key factors behind recent reductions in child poverty have been both rising employment levels (primarily promoted by UK policy, but supported by devolved employability and childcare-related policy) and the development of means-tested tax credits aimed at families both in and out of work (again reserved policy, but supported by devolved policy to improve advice provision). Tax credits are a key lever behind the reduction in child poverty in families with work *and* those without. However, through well publicised failings in the system, too many claimants have faced hardship through no fault of their own. Indeed, one out of five entitled families, including one in ten of the most deprived, miss out on tax credits worth £110 million in Scotland alone.[6] There has been a limited redistribution of income to the poorest, but with n an overall policy environment that has not challenged the incomes of the richest.

Despite the national minimum wage and tax credits, low pay, job insecurity, lack of flexibility for working parents, and sparse in-work support for those with disability or long-term illness continue to undermine work as a route out of poverty. Over half of children living in poverty are in households in which an adult is working;[7] a couple with two children and one partner working 40 hours a week for the national minimum wage, who receive full benefit and tax credit entitlements, are still left £50 per week below the poverty line.[8]

Furthermore, 30 per cent of poverty pay in Scotland is in the public sector, over which the devolved administration has direct responsibility.[9] Despite policy action aimed at improving employability and in-work progression, the Executive has failed to resolve the irony of promoting progressive anti-poverty strategies on one hand while paying poverty wages on the other. Affordable childcare provision is another key to overcoming barriers to employment. Despite significant improvements, childcare is still not accessible to many families, with a patchwork pattern of provision reflecting national targeting of resources and local prioritisation (Chapter 1).

Devolved policy to tackle poverty by improving the school attainment levels of the most disadvantaged, and so tackle the deficit of opportunity they face, has had little impact to date.[10] Furthermore, there is, as yet, no clear means of evaluating the impact on child poverty of targeting support at integrated children's services and care leavers. The *Hungry for Success* approach to improving child health through school nutrition has improved quality, but a highly targeted means-tested approach still leaves over 70,000 children in poverty without a free school meal.[11]

Towards the eradication of child poverty: a policy prescription for the future?

In Scotland, child poverty is falling in line with initial UK government targets. Yet extensive analysis shows that relying on current policy would see progress grind to a halt.[12] For families furthest below the poverty line, progress is already extremely limited.[13]

Modelling suggests that rising employment will now have a limited impact on child poverty.[14] Indeed, evidence from people experiencing poverty, indicates that low-quality, low-paid work may actually damage the lives of children by exacerbating the impact of parental ill-health and disability, and increasing family stress.[15] Nevertheless, ministers remain bullish in their focus on work as the solution to poverty.

The limitations of targeted approaches to tackling child poverty are also becoming apparent. Far too many families in poverty miss out on, or have to repay, vital tax credits; parents are still unable to access affordable childcare because they fall outside current targeted initiatives; and tens of thousands of children living in poverty do not receive free school meals.

So what policy changes are needed if further progress is to be made toward abolishing child poverty in Scotland?

First, action to increase the employment rate of parents needs to focus on tackling the low pay, insecurity, discrimination and family-unfriendly practice that too often make work an ineffective route out of poverty.

Second, the focus on work needs to be balanced by increases in the benefit and tax credit package for families who are not in a position to access paid employment.

Third, the limits of a targeted approach need to be recognised. Policy must rebalance the need to target resources with the need to ensure support reaches all families who need it. Childcare strategy must build on current patchwork improvements toward a policy of universal childcare, free at the point of delivery. Similarly, school meals policy needs to build on the improvement in nutritional quality toward a more universal free school meal approach.

Finally, serious consideration of the role income inequality plays in undermining progress toward the elimination of child poverty is urgently needed. It is noticeable that those countries which have low levels of child poverty also have more equal income distribution.[16] Scotland faces some fundamental choices. What kind of society do we want our children to grow up in? One that encourages the unrestrained growth of incomes for the few, but is scarred by continuing child poverty, or one that values all our children over the desire for ever lower taxes?

Notes

1 Scottish Executive, *Households Below Average Income 2004/05*, 2006, available online at: http://www.scotland.gov.uk/Publications/2006/03/08155404/0; Child Poverty Action Group, *Poverty: the stats*, 2006

2 J Bradshaw, *A Review of the Comparative Evidence on Child Poverty*, Joseph Rowntree Foundation, 2006

3 Scottish Executive, *Closing the Opportunity Gap*, available online at: http://www.scotland.gov.uk/Topics/People/Social-Inclusion/17415/opportunity

4 See note 3

5 Expert Panel on School Meals, *Hungry for Success: a whole school approach to school meals in Scotland*, 2006, available online at: http://www.scotland. gov.uk/Topics/Education/Schools/HLivi/schoolmeals/hungry-for-success

6 Child Poverty Action Group Press Release, 6 March 2006

7 Department for Work and Pensions, *Households Below Average Income 2004/05*, Corporate Document Services, 2006

8 J Bradshaw, *Understanding and Overcoming Poverty*, keynote address to JRF centenary conference, 2005, available online at: http://www.jrf.org.uk/confer ences/centenary/presentations.asp

9 G Palmer, J Carr and P Kenway, *Monitoring Poverty and Social Exclusion in Scotland 2005*, Joseph Rowntree Foundation, 2005, available online at: http://www.poverty.org.uk/reports/scotland%202005%20findings.pdf

10 See note 3

11 CPAG in Scotland internal analysis: 23 per cent of children are living in poverty (see note 1) yet only 13 per cent get a free school meal; Scottish Executive, *School Meals in Scotland 2006*, available online at: http://www.scotland.gov.uk/ Publications/2006/06/05141444/1

12 D Hirsch, *What Will it Take to End Child Poverty? Firing on all cylinders*, Joseph Rowntree Foundation, 2006

13 Save the Children, *The Government's Invisible Million: Britain's poorest children*, 2006, available online at: http://www.savethechildren.org.uk/scuk_cache/ scuk/cache/cmsattach/3794_BPC2Briefing.pdf

14 See note 13

15 G Preston (ed), *A Route Out of Poverty? Disabled people, work and welfare reform*, CPAG, 2006; L Payne, *Unequal Choices*, End Child Poverty, 2006

16 B Jackson and P Siegal, *Why Inequality Matters?*, Catalyst Working Paper, 2004

Twelve

Lone-parent families

Marion Davis

There is a wide diversity of family arrangements in contemporary Scotland, including married couples with children, cohabiting couples with children, lone parents, families reconstituted by remarriage, families reconstituted through cohabitation, families headed by gay and lesbian parents, separated or divorced parents who share parenting responsibilities, and family units living with extended family in the same household. We are now more likely to acknowledge this diversity, although there have always been different shapes and sizes of families influenced by economic and personal circumstances, and the social and cultural patterns of the time and place. Whatever their composition, families should be treated as being equally valid and should be equally valued. To achieve a socially inclusive society, we must seek to overcome family poverty, which diminishes life chances and restricts aspirations, with consequences that echo down the years in the lives of parents and their children. In this chapter, we pay particular attention to the family poverty that is experienced in lone-parent households.

Family poverty in Scotland

Whether a family is able to meet the material needs of children depends more on whether it has income from work than on whether it has two parents. The much greater amount of time that lone parents spend out of paid work means that they are more often caught in a 'hardship trap'. As the majority of lone-parent households are women, this burden hits harder on women than men. More generally, research shows that the weight of responsibility for overseeing family finances in low-income families falls on women. Thus, women's poverty is inevitably linked with that of children. Policy makers, it is argued, must acknowledge this link in their efforts to eradicate child poverty.[1]

The economic position of families strongly affects the present and future welfare of children. Today's high level of child poverty is likely to have continuing negative effects on families as the present generation grows up. Equally, any measures that successfully address child poverty, especially by giving more of today's parents access to employment, are likely to have wide-ranging effects in the years ahead that go beyond the improvement of the immediate welfare of children living in poverty.[2]

Almost half of all (both workless and working) lone parents in Scotland are living with income poverty; almost three times the rate for couples with children. A major reason for this is the high levels of worklessness; around half of lone parents are working and half are not.[3] In terms of income level, 66 per cent of lone-parent families in Scotland live on an income of less than £15,000 compared with 11 per cent of two-parent families. There is a huge gap in experience between lone parents and partnered women – 49 per cent of women in lone-parent households are in employment, compared with 71 per cent of women in two-parent family households.[4]

Policy developments

Family policy is a cross-cutting issue that is dispersed across several policy areas, such as education, health, social security, employment, social services and housing, and spans both devolved and reserved policy areas of the Scottish Executive and UK Parliament. A family's access to resources is principally reliant on their earned income and/or state benefits. These are, to a great extent, affected by Westminster macro-policies in relation to the economy, employment and income redistribution.[5] There are four broad goals of the Government's strategy to tackle family poverty.

- 'Work for those who can', helping parents participate in the labour market. This includes an overall target of an 80 per cent employment rate and a specific lone-parent target of 70 per cent.
- Financial support for families, with more support for those who need it most.
- Excellent public services that improve children's life chances and break cycles of deprivation.
- Support for parents in their parenting role so they can guide their children through life transitions.[6]

A range of policies have been developed to support the UK Government achieve these goals – for example, tax credits, the national minimum wage, welfare to work initiatives and work/life balance policies (making work pay), and enhanced rates of child benefit, child tax credit, savings and asset-ownership policies (financial support).[7]

Devolution means that Scottish family policy has the potential for divergence from Westminster.[8] Relevant anti-poverty and social inclusion policy agendas include: *Closing the Opportunity Gap*; *Workforce Plus*; *Meeting the Childcare Challenge: a childcare strategy for Scotland*; Working for Families initiatives; early education for three- and four-year-olds; and Sure Start services.[9] Much of this Scottish agenda for over-coming family poverty mirrors that of the UK agenda, for example, with regards to childcare and education.

Emerging issues

Lone parents are one of the groups targeted by the range of welfare-to-work reforms.[10] However, attaining targets on lone parents' employment and tackling social exclusion will not be achieved by simply carrying forward current policies. The key issues which must be addressed are:

- high level of economic disadvantage among those out of 'work';
- financial insecurity in an out of employment;
- high and increasing housing and childcare costs;
- low pay–high turnover economy;
- work–family balance (balancing caring work and employment);
- local opportunities and other 'local' factors;
- multi-dimensional poverty (income poverty and time poverty as separate issues).

The current policy model in the UK and European Union is that of the 'adult worker' model.[11] Through this, parents are to be encouraged to work and their caring responsibilities are to be shared with formal service providers of childcare. This assumes that formal care is sufficient, viable, desired and effective, ignores the intimate nature of parenting and penalises those who parent/care. A move towards an 'individual worker/carer' model, such as that progressed in countries such as New Zealand and Norway, would support lone parents into employment only when their individual circumstances and parental responsibilities allow, and would facilitate a lone-parent strategy which is part of a wider family policy that seeks to reconcile increased women's employment with time for parental childcare.[12]

Childcare: the key to freeing families from poverty

The lack of affordable childcare in the UK and Scotland means that many families are still trapped in a life of low income and low expectations. With fewer families now living in poverty and thousands of new childcare places created, the childcare strategy has made positive progress. However, further development of government childcare policy is required if all families are to have the chance of a life free from poverty.

Childcare provision is often patchy, inflexible and expensive, preventing women from returning to work or forcing them to work fewer hours to fit around it. Mothers working part time have average hourly earnings only 59 per cent of men working full time. For most women, fewer hours limit training opportunities and chances of promotion, and mean lower pay and inadequate pension provision.[13] There is a need to work toward equality of opportunity and provision across Scotland.[14]

The link between poverty and diminished life chances for parents and children calls for creative strategies by the UK, Scottish and local government to address the issues that trap families in poverty and social exclusion. We must guard against further demonising those families by blaming people for their circumstances and pursuing punitive policies.[15] A key to future success is the need to differentiate between welfare which imposes 'sanctions' and welfare which offers 'incentives'. Supporting people to gain rewarding work appropriate to their circumstances has benefits for all, but welfare-to-work provisions at present appear to be a discipline imposed on those families already beleaguered by disadvantage.

Notes

1   R Lister, 'The Links Between Women's and Children's Poverty', *Poverty* 121, CPAG, 2005
2   P Gregg, S Harkness and S Machin, *Child Development and Family Income*, Joseph Rowntree Foundation,1999
3   New Policy Institute, *Monitoring Poverty and Social Exclusion in Scotland*, 2005
4   Scottish Executive, *Scotland's People: Annual Report 2005*, 2006
5   E Minoff, *The UK Commitment: ending child poverty by 2020*, Center for Law

and Social Policy, 2006

6 Department for Work and Pensions, *Opportunity for All: seventh annual report*, The Stationery Office, 2005, available online at: http://www.dwp.gov.uk/media-centre/pressreleases/2005/oct/ofa7.PDF

7 HM Treasury, *Child Poverty Review*, The Stationery Office, 2004, available online at: http://www.hm-treasury.gov.uk/spending_review/spend_sr04/associated_documents/spending_sr04_childpoverty.cfm

8 F Wasoff and M Hill, *Family Policy in Scotland*, Centre for Research on Families and Relationships Research Briefing No. 3, 2002

9 Scottish Executive, *Closing the Opportunity Gap*, 2005 and *Workforce Plus: an employability framework for Scotland,* 2006

10 Department for Work and Pensions, *A New Deal For Welfare: empowering people to work*, The Stationery Office, 2006, available online at: http://www.dwp.gov.uk/welfarereform/legislation_green_paper.asp

11 J Lewis, 'Individualisation: assumptions about the existence of an adult worker model and the shift towards contractualism', in A Carling, S Duncan and R Edwards (eds), *Analysing Families: morality and rationality in policy and practice*, Routledge, 2002

12 J Millar and M Evans, *Lone Parents and Employment: international comparisons of what works*, CASP for DWP, 2003

13 H Land, *Women, Child Poverty and Childcare: making the links*, The Daycare Trust and the TUC, 2004

14 JH McKendrick, S Cunningham-Burley and K Backett-Milburn, *Life In Low-income Families in Scotland*, Scottish Executive, 2003

15 T Blair MP, *Poverty and Social Exclusion: a lecture by Tony Blair*, Joseph Rowntree Foundation, 2006

Thirteen
Childless adults
Robin Tennant

Introduction

The majority of working-age adults living with poverty in Scotland live in households without children. Indeed, one in every six working-age adults living without children in Scotland is currently living with income poverty (16 per cent – see Table 4.3). They are no less likely to be living in poverty than they were in the mid-1990s. However, as the numbers of adults living alone has increased over the corresponding period, the number of working-age adults without dependent children who are living in income poverty has increased to around 400,000 at the current time.[1] The majority of single adult households are headed by men; while 13 per cent of adult men live in such households, the corresponding figure for women is 8 per cent.[2]

Yet the rise in single adult poverty would appear to be counter intuitive. Employment rates in Scotland have risen significantly since 1997; these rates have not only caught up with, but have overtaken, those of the UK. Since 1998, there has been a net gain of over 196,000 jobs in the Scottish economy.[3] So why is poverty among working-age adults without children increasing, in an era of substantial economic growth and a strong policy emphasis on work as the key route out of poverty?

Policy

The UK government and the Scottish Executive have pledged to eradicate *child* poverty. Targets and indicators have been set against which to measure progress (see Chapter 11). There have also been a number of policy initiatives to help older people, most notably the introduction of pension credit in October 2003. The proportion of pensioners living in relative low-income households has almost halved since 1996/97 (see Table 4.1).

However, while there have been specific policies and targets for child poverty, and broad aims for pensioner poverty, there have been no equivalent targets, aspirations or specific policies to reduce poverty among working-age adults without children. Out-of-work benefits for adults without children, even accounting for inflation, have effectively been frozen since 1997, compared with a rise of just over 33 per cent for both households with dependent children and pensioners.[4] Working tax credit has extended 'in-work' support to reach some groups of working-age adults without children. However, this and other policies aimed at working-age adults (such as the national minimum wage, and the New Deal for Young People) have not guaranteed income levels above poverty rates.

Single adult living and the world of work

According to recent research, 43 per cent of people who become single-person households experience a drop in income; single-person households also face higher living costs in that they cannot share the costs of rent, council tax, utilities and food; and people living alone face greater labour market risks (multi-person households are more likely to have at least one person working, and are less susceptible to redundancy or unemployment).[5]

While many people have benefited from policies and a booming economy, evidence suggests that those benefiting are those who would have had little trouble re-entering the labour market anyway. Those not benefiting from current government strategies include older workers whose skills may have become redundant, people with low skills and qualifications, homeless people (over the period 1995–2005, the number of single-adult households in Scotland becoming homeless rose by a half), people recovering from drug and alcohol abuse, former prostitutes, people with a history of mental and physical ill-health (80 per cent of working-age people in Scotland receiving a key out-of-work benefit for two years or more are sick or disabled) and ex-offenders.[6]

These groups face *significant* barriers to entering the labour market. For example, the majority of employers have been found to '... deliberately exclude[d] people with certain characteristics – such as a criminal record, a history of alcohol or drug dependence or long-term sickness, and homelessness – when recruiting staff', and that '... 55 per cent of employers . . . stated that nothing would persuade them to recruit the core jobless'.[7] In addition, many in the 'core-groups' above are seen as politically contentious or as the undeserving poor.[8] Other barriers can include lack of in-work support that can deal with their health needs, lack of appropriate training and employment opportunities, and getting caught up in the poverty/benefits trap if they take a low-paid job.

Because of the barriers they face in entering the labour market, not only are their prospects for escaping poverty poorer in the short term, given the policy emphasis on 'work as the key route out of poverty', their situation is compounded by erosions in the value of their welfare benefits.

What is on offer in the world of work?

The nature of many of the jobs created over recent years in Scotland are in areas and sectors notorious for low pay, low skills and lack of security. Increases have overwhelmingly taken place in the service sector, with manufacturing and agriculture continuing to show a decline in employment levels.[9]

A significant element of service sector employment growth has been part-time employment carried out by women. Between 1998 and 2002, part-time jobs in the service sector grew by 53 per cent. According to the Scottish Executive, 'The growth in part-time employment in all sectors is strong over the period and this is particularly pronounced in the service sector' and 'The fall in the economic inactivity rate for working age individuals is largely attributable to women, with the male rate moving in the same direction, though at a significantly reduced rate'.[10] Women's employment rates in the Scotland are at their highest since 1984. Given household trends and policy emphases, it is likely that most of this activity is benefiting adults living in households with children.

Work is not necessarily an escape route from poverty for single adults. As Howarth and Kenway note, ' . . . too much of the burden of addressing low pay has been left to the minimum wage'.[11] In other words, while the national minimum wage may have tackled the worst excesses of low pay, the minimum wage is not an anti-poverty wage. Estimates vary, but an anti-poverty pay should be at least £7 to £8 per hour as advocated by the London Citizens' Living Wage campaigns.[12] The European Decency Threshold, as advocated by the Scottish Low Pay Unit, is £6.70 per hour. These are far in excess of the £5.35 per hour minimum wage at the time of writing. Rather than having a steppingstone to a better future, people can become trapped in low-paid, dead end jobs that do little to tackle the poverty they face.

Insecurity in employment should also be noted; 50 per cent of men and 33 per cent of women making a new claim for jobseeker's allowance were claiming six months before.[13] An insecure working environment and low levels of pay represent yet more barriers to escaping poverty for the vulnerable groups above as they can get caught in a vicious 'low pay-no pay' cycle.

Conclusion

This chapter has explored the poverty among working-age adults without children. It has argued that there are significant barriers to be tackled if poverty is to be reduced among single working-age adults. It is vital that: we begin to target reductions in the level and intensity of poverty; their situation is fully understood; and specific and *appropriate* policy interventions are developed. Policy makers should be: raising the level of welfare benefits as a necessary first step; increasing social support programmes to pave the way for people in these 'core groups' to rebuild their lives; challenging discrimination among employers; and creating appropriate, fulfilling and well-paid employment.

While welfare benefits and the national minimum wage are reserved issues (although arguably the Scottish Parliament and Executive have an advocacy role to play here), there are areas in which the Scottish Executive can play a meaningful role in reducing poverty among adults without children. For example, reform or replacement of the council tax (to make paying for public services more progressive) in a way that would exempt people on low pay or benefits would increase the income in peoples' pockets; widening the concessionary fare scheme beyond pensioners; developing an extensive social housing building programme; increasing funding for social support programmes that tackle issues such as rehabilitation of offenders, mental health, drug and alcohol abuse and homelessness; and challenging discrimination and negative attitudes among employers and the wider public through public awareness initiatives like those adopted to tackle racism.

Notes

1   J Bennett and M Dixon, *Single Adult Households and Social Policy: looking forward*, Joseph Rowntree Foundation, 2006

2   C Martin and others, *Scotland's People: Annual Report from the 2003/04 Scottish Household Survey*, Scottish Executive, 2006, p11, Table 3.8

3   Scottish Executive, *Scottish Economic Report*, 2005

4   See note 2

5   See note 1

6   C Howarth and P Kenway, *Monitoring Poverty and Social Exclusion in Scotland*, Joseph Rowntree Foundation/New Policy Institute, 2005; J Adams, *Towards Full Employment: tackling economic inactivity*, Institute for Public Policy Research, 2006

7   CIPD, *Labour Market Outlook; Survey Report*, Summer/Autumn 2005.

8   P Spicker, *Poverty and the Welfare State: dispelling the myths*, Catalyst, 2002

9   See note 2

10 See note 2

11 C Howarth and P Kenaway, *Why Worry Any More About the Low Paid*, New Policy Institute, 2005

12 London Citizens, *Low Wage Campaign*, available online at: http://www.livingwage.org.uk/

13 See note 12

Fourteen

Addressing poverty in Scotland from an anti-racist perspective: impact on visible minority ethnic communities

Tesfu Gessesse

This chapter endeavours to address the contemporary discourse about poverty in Scotland, from an anti-racist, community-based perspective. The intention is to explore the impact of recent national policy-related initiatives that are relevant to the reduction of poverty and social exclusion on the day-to-day lives of visible minority ethnic communities, and to prescribe what needs to be done in the future.[1] This is important, as the rate of poverty in Scotland is far greater among minority ethnic groups than white populations, at each stage in the life cycle (see Table 4.10).

Poverty and racial inequality

Although social class continues to be the dominant analytical factor in contemporary debates about poverty, there is now greater recognition that other social factors have a determining effect on particular groups in Scottish society. The audit of research by Netto and others highlighted the different impact that poverty has on visible minority ethnic groups; institutionalised racial discrimination that is endemic across welfare services; and the compounding difficulties that these communities experience because of the effects of multiple-discrimination.[2] This shift towards a more broad-based understanding of poverty was an important change within the Scottish context, as it demonstrated the need to recognise how systemic barriers within existing public services can exclude visible ethnic minorities as actual beneficiaries from poverty reduction strategies and polices.

So what has changed since 2002 to secure a more racially inclusive society in Scotland, or since the last edition of *Poverty in Scotland* was published? The Scottish Executive has promoted applied research, policies and other initiatives, which have been designed to benefit minority ethnic communities in Scotland. An attempt has been made to examine three key areas of national activity which, when taken together, have the potential to reduce poverty and enhance social inclusion; an overview of what has been achieved in each of these fields will be presented; and a suggestion from a community-based perspective will be made where further efforts are required.

Policy, statistical data and research

In response to the report of the Stephen Lawrence Inquiry, the Scottish Executive established the Race Equality Advisory Forum (REAF) with the remit to advise on policy and strategy. REAF consulted widely with minority ethnic communities and recommended 17 action points for implementation.[3] Thus far, the Scottish Executive has attempted to address at least nine of these, namely: race equality training; public appointments; improved research, information and statistics on minority ethnic people in Scotland; reporting on the promotion of race equality; multi-agency working; education; health and social care; social inclusion; and voluntary sector issues.

It is fair to say that the progress achieved represents a fair start and a commitment by the Scottish Executive to ensure that race equality is now firmly on the agenda in Scotland. However, it is important to recognise that even in the above areas, there is much to be done to achieve sustainable change and that the key recommendations, which are completely neglected at the moment, are equally, if not more, crucial to alleviate poverty within the minority ethnic communities – for example, mainstreaming race equality into planning, policy design and service delivery; employment in the public sector; translation and interpreting; consultation with minority ethnic communities; and enterprise and lifelong learning.

In terms of improved statistical databases concerning racial and religious diversity, the Scottish Executive has taken steps to ensure that statistical information is available for public service planning and accountability. This is an important change, given the emphasis on removing institutional barriers and the significant growth in the size of the minority ethnic population in Scotland.

The scope and quality of race-related research has also increased, starting with the audit of research by Netto and others.[4] A range of studies in education, housing, health and related fields, all of which form a national resource base to guide policy and practice, has also been undertaken across Scotland.

Minority ethnic health

Health inequality within minority ethnic communities has been acknowledged over the past decade; for example, recent research by the University of Edinburgh found that the incidence of heart attacks among Scots of Indian and Pakistani origin is 60–70 per cent higher than among with non-South Asians.[5] Reasons for this are believed to include generally poorer socio-economic status, genetic and environmental factors, and barriers to accessing health services due to the effects of racism. Many minority ethnic organisations in Scotland report that although there is improvement in the collection of data, much remains to be done. Issues of interpreting and translation, medical privacy, and the cultural appropriateness of healthcare services still remain as priority health issues for minority ethnic communities in Scotland.

In 2002, the Scottish Executive launched Fair for All, its strategic response for health improvement. It established the National Resource Centre For Ethnic Minorities in Health:

> ... to help to ensure a quality service that addresses the concerns of marginalised minority ethnic communities and to facilitate the development of a sensitive and culturally competent service based on anti-discriminatory policies and practices.[6]

Alongside this, all health boards were required to develop strategic action plans to address minority ethnic health inequalities.

Health issues remain a major concern for minority ethnic communities and it will require concerted efforts for another decade before any objective assessment of the effectiveness of these initiatives can be made.

Educational attainment and employment

Educational attainment and employment are inter-related factors and central to the reduction of poverty for all communities. Recent research has shown that Scottish schools have yet to meet the expectations of minority ethnic children and their families because of the ways in which they are organised, the curriculum and the absence of a multi-racial workforce.[7] Parents complain about racism and bullying from as early as nursery stage and the inability of primary schoolteachers to challenge racism. At secondary school level, many minority ethnic pupils report that they are systematically excluded from getting appropriate advice, support and guidance about their education. The Black Community Development Project has two youth groups and when six minority ethnic secondary school pupils were asked about their experience of high school, their collective response can be summarised as follows:

> 'When we started S1 it was OK as it was the first year of high school life. However, when we reached S2, no one has told us that we have to work harder at S2, as the results at S2 will determine whether we will be studying for Credit, Standard, or Foundation courses when it comes to doing our Standard Grade. Our parents go to parents' night but they do not know what to ask, as they do not understand the education system. The school never organises interpreters.'

With a higher risk of parents not having the information to guide pupils, it is imperative that schools give unequivocal guidance to give all pupils the same chance to succeed. The parents of gypsy/traveller children have expressed similar criticisms.[3]

In terms of employment, recent research by the Equal Opportunities Commission for Scotland reported that economic activity among minority ethnic women is significantly lower than among white women: for Caribbean women 65 per cent; African and Indian women 56 per cent; Chinese women 52 per cent; Pakistani and Bangladeshi women drop to 35 per cent.[9] Scottish minority ethnic business owners account for 3 per cent of all self-employed in the nation; many say that they were forced to become self-employed, as all the doors for employment were closed for them.

Agenda for the future

As highlighted above, the twin goals of poverty reduction and anti-racism are inextricably linked, with visible minority ethnic groups, many of whom live in poverty (Table 4.10), excluded or invisible in democratic life. To date, the Scottish Parliament has shown encouraging signs that it is committed to tackling racial discrimination in Scotland. If there is a desire to create a just and harmonious society in Scotland, there needs to be a genuine commitment by policy makers to continue to:

- engage with visible minority ethnic communities in all aspects of policy development regarding social, economic, political participation;
- allocate resources based on needs and a targeted approach to balance current inequalities between groups in society;
- ensure that the culture and workforce of public institutions, including of the Scottish Executive and Parliament, change to reflect the diverse society within Scotland.

Notes

1   For the purpose of this article, 'visible minority ethnic communities' refers to those peoples whose ethnic origins are mainly from Africa and the Caribbean, Asia, and South America; it acknowledges the significance that colour and physical appearance play in the experience of racial discrimination.

2   G Netto, R Arshad, P de Lima, F Almeida Diniz, M MacEwan, V Patel and R Syed, *Audit of Research on Minority Ethnic Issues in Scotland from a 'Race' Perspective*, Scottish Executive Central Research Unit, 2001

3   Scottish Executive, *Making it Real: a race equality strategy for Scotland*, The Stationery Office, 2002

4   See note 2

5   R Bhopal, 'What is the Risk of Coronary Heart Disease in South Asians? A review of UK research', *Journal of Public Health Medicine*, Vol 22, pp375–85, 2000, available online at: http://www.jpubhealth.oxfordjournals.org/cgi/content/abstract/22/3/375

6   National Resource Centre for Ethnic Minorities in Health, *Annual Report*, 2003

7   R Arshad, F Almeida Diniz, E Kelly, P O'Hara, S Sharp and R Syed, *Minority Ethnic Pupils' Experience of Schools in Scotland*, The Stationery Office, 2004

8   Blake Stevenson Ltd, *Focus Group with Minority Ethnic Communities*, Scottish Executive Central Research Unit, 2003

9   Equal Opportunities Commission Scotland, *Moving on Up? Visible minority ethnic women at work*, EOC, 2006

Fifteen
Asylum seekers
Mhoraig Green and Mick Doyle

Introduction

In recent years, asylum seekers in the UK have become increasingly socially excluded as a result of government policy.[1] The fact that asylum seekers are not entitled to work, and can claim only very limited benefits, leads many observers to conclude that the UK government is using poverty as a lever to deter people from claiming asylum here and to force refused asylum seekers to return home 'voluntarily'. Since asylum continues to be a reserved matter, asylum seekers living in Scotland largely remain at the mercy of Westminster policy makers. This chapter focuses on examples of recent UK policy.

Scotland has a combined asylum-seeker and refugee population of roughly 10,000 people. Currently, around 6,000 of these are asylum seekers awaiting a decision for what can be an extended period. There are also a significant number of refused asylum seekers who have been left fully destitute by the state, with no support and no right to work to support themselves and their dependants.

Glasgow remains the only city in Scotland directly supporting asylum seekers in significant numbers and is the largest site for the dispersal programme outside London. Support networks began to develop when people first arrived in 2001.[2] However, these are primarily comprised of voluntary sector organisations and people from the communities in which asylum seekers live. In practice, when the state refuses to support an asylum seeker, that person becomes dependent on the unsustainable support of charities, friends and neighbours, who in general are living in some of the most deprived communities in Scotland.[3]

Main policy developments

Several major pieces of asylum legislation and policy have created poverty among asylum seekers. Perhaps most significantly, since June 2002, asylum seekers have been refused permission to work for the duration of their asylum application. Many households in Glasgow have waited several years for their asylum applications to be resolved. This policy also affects the future employability of people granted refugee status and contributes to the often serious and debilitating poverty they face.

Restricting access to the labour market forces asylum seekers to live on support from the Immigration and Nationality Directorate–Scottish Asylum Support Service (IND/SASS); this was formerly known as the National Asylum Support Service (NASS), paid at 30 per cent below the rate of income support. The costs of asylum seekers' housing and utility bills are met by IND/SASS and, while this restricts the control they have over their income, it does avoid problems such as fuel poverty, although there is emerging evidence that this can lead to major fuel poverty problems for refugees who get leave to remain in the UK and suddenly find themselves faced with fuel bills – often in hard-to-heat homes.

The Immigration, Nationality and Asylum Act 2002 gave the UK government the power to refuse to support an asylum seeker if s/he had failed to claim asylum as soon as s/he arrived in the country (section 55). This Act penalised people for their lack of knowledge of the requirements of a foreign legal system, rather than the merits of their claim for asylum.[4] The provision led to around a hundred people being made homeless and destitute in Scotland during 2004, whilst also unable to work to support themselves. However, following successful legal challenges, this power is now significantly limited.

Ostensibly, these policies are designed to ensure that people do not take advantage of the asylum system for economic reasons. Support, however, has been restricted to a level where people genuinely fleeing persecution are forced to live in poverty in Scotland while their asylum application is assessed. Asylum seekers in Scotland also live in fear of the implementation of a raft of un-enacted legislation, including the power to make families with children homeless and destitute.

If someone is refused asylum they face even more severe poverty. They may be entitled to support under section 4 of the Immigration and Asylum Act 1999 while they pursue a judicial review or wait to return home. However, this provision is very limited and typically comprises shared accommodation with mostly voucher support or full board meals. This is despite the fact that vouchers were theoretically abolished in 2002, on the grounds that they were stigmatising.[5] The Immigration and Asylum Act 2004 also introduced a provision that made this support conditional on participation in community service. However, the Government was unable to find partners who would participate and, therefore, this provision has not been implemented.

Most people are only eligible to apply for section 4 support if they are willing to return home, but many refused asylum seekers are unwilling or unable to return home and, therefore, are left with no support and no right to work.[6] Many countries are unsafe (for example, Iraq and Somalia) or will not issue return travel documents (for example, China) and there is no suitable long-term provision for refused asylum seekers from these places. Some people go underground immediately after receiving a negative decision, placing themselves and their families in destitution because they fear return and have no confidence that the UK asylum system will provide protection. The failures of the asylum system are well documented.[7]

Impact and responses

Many traditional anti-poverty responses are simply ineffective with asylum seekers. For example, there is no value in targeted benefit take-up campaigns since they have no significant entitlements to highlight. Community development responses to poverty are also problematic. Credit union development among asylum-seeker populations, for example, is difficult to envisage, given their meagre incomes and the threat of removal from the UK at extremely short notice. Work to improve the employability of individuals has limited impact in the short to medium term while people are denied access to work.

The communities where asylum seekers live, despite being poor themselves, have reached out to support people fleeing persecution. These communities have developed localised welfare alternatives to support asylum-seeking friends and neighbours who have been evicted or denied benefits. Hence, we now see the collection of food and money by individuals, churches and community groups, and volunteers being asked to accommodate refused asylum seekers in their own homes for indefinite periods. Communities continue to respond by distributing humanitarian aid to new arrivals, including food, clothing and household goods.

Existing provision for destitute people in Scotland is not always suitable for asylum seekers at the end of the process: some have reported receiving hostile and frightening reception from other users of soup kitchens and homeless shelters. Destitute asylum seekers often turn to members of their community for support, either other asylum seekers or Scottish friends. Some communities are responding to this by setting up dry food stores and local hardship funds. However, these informal solutions are not sustainable and often involve the poor sustaining the desperately poor in a system more reminiscent of the nineteenth, than the twenty-first, century.

Since the experiences of this group are so radically different from those of other poorer sections of UK society, it seems that a key element of any anti-poverty response must be to raise awareness. This is crucial for community groups and campaigning organisations who could highlight these injustices, promote solidarity and demand more civilised treatment of asylum seekers, which is at least comparable with other groups experiencing poverty in the UK.

Recommendations

Three main policy platforms could be used to unite pro-asylum seeker and anti-poverty campaigners. The first is the principle of full support, at the same level as UK benefit claimants, until the point of removal from the UK. It is surely unacceptable that anyone in contemporary Scotland should be deliberately denied the basic means of existence. Furthermore, this would reduce the likelihood of failed asylum seekers engaging in illegal work, often facilitated by criminal elements.

The second is that there should be a concerted effort to eradicate accidental administrative destitution. Recent research confirms that destitution as a result of system failures is significant.[8] Access to emergency payments should be as robust as those in place for other benefit recipients. At present, individuals and families wait too long for problems to be effectively resolved. There is also some anecdotal evidence that these problems happen repeatedly.

Perhaps more controversially, the policy which denies people the right to work must be reconsidered. The European reception directive requires countries to grant permission to work for those with no initial decision on their claim within one year. However, in Scotland most people receive an initial refusal quickly and then languish in the appeals process, sometimes for several years, with no right to work. In our view, this directive should be amended to allow those with no final decision after one year to be awarded permission to work. Asylum seekers who cannot be removed from the country should be permitted to work and support themselves when they have no access to benefits, as is already the case in some other European countries.

The aspirations of the Scottish Parliament to eradicate poverty are being compromised by an asylum process that uses poverty as a policy tool. This also undermines our international obligation to provide protection to people fleeing persecution. As it stands, the poverty endured by asylum seekers in Scotland is a national disgrace.

Notes

1   J Hills and K Stewart (eds), *A More Equal Society? New Labour, poverty, inequality and exclusion*, The Policy Press, 2005
2   K Wren, *Building Bridges: local responses to the resettlement of asylum seekers in Glasgow*, Scottish Centre for Research on Social Justice, 2004
3   M Green, *They Think We Are Nothing: a survey of destitute asylum seekers and refugees in Scotland*, Scottish Refugee Council, 2006
4   Inter-agency Partnership, *The Impact of Section 55 on the Inter-agency Partnership and the Asylum Seekers it Supports*, 2004
5   Immigration Nationality Directorate, *Report of the Operational Reviews of the Voucher and Dispersal Schemes of the National Asylum Support Service*, Home Office, 2001
6   See note 3
7   See for example, S Cutler and M Wren, *Justice Denied: asylum and immigration aid – a system in crisis*, Asylum Aid and Bail for Immigration Detainees, 2005
8   See note 3

Sixteen

Community responses: poverty, childcare and mothers' transitions to work

Fiona Forsyth

Rosemount Lifelong Learning is a community-managed, anti-poverty organisation which provides high-quality childcare and lifelong learning opportunities for families from North Glasgow. Between 2002 and 2003, we were involved in a collaborative research project with the Scottish Poverty Information Unit and the Centre for Research into Families and Relationships, looking at the barriers women face moving from unemployment into sustainable employment. The research examined 'how care and financial issues impact on the process of transition, how strategies developed at a national level have been experienced by families within a specific locality and how community-based resources such as Rosemount Lifelong Learning can affect the impact of those policies'.[1] The research was funded by the European Social Fund, as part of a 'demonstration project' in order to inform local and European employment policy.

The research, which used several participatory methodologies, has yielded benefits for participants who gained skills which they were able to use in higher education and, in one case, to gain employment as a research assistant. It has had a demonstrable impact on policy development, especially the development of the Scottish Executive Working for Families programme and has helped Rosemount to develop innovative services in partnership with new stakeholders.

Findings

The research began by examining what is meant by care. Twelve women kept 'care diaries' for two weeks, in which they recorded details of the practical issues they faced organising formal and informal care. In subsequent interviews, they reflected on these diaries and on their views about care:[2]

> 'I would sort of think, you know, when I was writing things down, oh God, I didn't realise that I done so much, you know, in a day. It was trying to fit everything in...just sort of makes you look a lot differently at your life. I mean, 'cos when you're just going from day to day, you just take it for granted, you know, you do one day and the next day and you don't really think about it.'

The research showed the day-to-day reality of managing caring responsibilities on a low income, and the added complexity when women became involved in education or employment. It showed the importance of informal care from relatives, an issue which has received little consideration from policy makers, who tend to view formal and informal childcare as alternatives.

However, the widespread incidence of poor health meant that informal support networks tended to be very fragile.

> 'She's my main support, my Mum. I was never able to do anything without my Mum. But she's not fit enough now. She had an operation that went badly – although she would never say 'no', then I know her good days and her bad days and I would never pressurise her into, you know, if she was really unwell that day, then I wouldn't have been going over and I wouldn't have been at work, it's as simple as that.'

Coping with their own poor health and the health needs of those they cared for is a significant barrier to employment for many women.

The second study examined financial barriers experienced by women making transitions into employment or higher education, including lack of information about in-work benefits, delays in payments of tax credits and a lack of affordable nurseries, after-school care and breakfast clubs. There were many additional costs such as creditors' demands for repayment, costs of informal care, travel costs, prescription charges, school meals, packed lunches for themselves, school clothing, work clothes, and paying into 'worksheets' (for example, for when someone leaves work).

Surprisingly, the transition to full-time higher education was more problematic than the move into work. Women were extremely reluctant to come off benefits and take on student loans, incurring high levels of debt and losing access to housing benefit. Caring responsibilities tended to rule out the possibility of supplementing student loans through part-time jobs. The ideal solution was to find a part-time course and stay on benefits, but there were very few courses available at the right level, and these might be only available in the evenings.

> 'That's a problem because I've got to find somebody to watch [C] at night. I have been getting that but I'm going out at tea time and I'm not getting to put him down to bed, two nights a week. The full-time course would have been ideal – it was four full days, but it just wasn't working out for me financially, so I had to go part time. I don't like part time and I will be lucky if I can stick it because I can't cope with going out at 5 o'clock at night.'

Although the women in this research were critical of government policies, their personal goals were not any different to these, which aim to encourage mothers in low-income families to take up employment. They saw paid employment, or employment after further education, as a positive goal, which would bring rewards for them and for their families. However, in practice, all of the women in the study found it very difficult to carry out their plans because of the difficulties in combining paid employment and care.

Impact on policy: to launch two Working for Families pilot projects

On 1 September 2003, Communities Minister Margaret Curran came to Rosemount Lifelong Learning to launch two Working for Families pilot projects:

> 'Innovative projects such as Rosemount Transitions will give these parents greater opportunities to work and learn, while their children are cared for in a safe environment. Next year, parents across Scotland will benefit from similar projects, as a result of the £20 million investment we have allocated for this purpose.'[3]

The Rosemount Transitions project, which implemented the recommendations of the earlier research, created a four-person information, support and guidance service with a wide remit. Issues presented by service users included health, addictions, bereavement, children's behaviour, domestic violence, rape, debt, benefits, childcare, bursaries and student loans, study skills, application forms and bullying at work.

From 2004, Working for Families initiatives were developed across ten local authorities in Scot and with high levels of child poverty.[4] One of these initiatives was the (Rosemount) HNC pilot project, developed by a partnership of Glasgow City Council, Jobcentre Plus and Rosemount Lifelong Learning specifica ly to address the barriers to full-time higher education, identified in our research. In 2005/06, 22 parents attended full-time HNC courses at five colleges in Glasgow, remaining on benefits and receiving childcare support, the majority of whom graduated in July 2006. The success of this project demonstrates the advantages of removing benefits traps, as described by one of the earlier research participants:

> 'Anybody that's going into college or university that have children, they should get free childcare. In the long run, these people are going there to get an education, so when they're coming back out, they are going to put money back into the system through their national insurance and so on when they have their qualification.'

Rosemount staff, directors and service users are pleased to see positive results from the disseminat on of our research, especially where this leads to policy initiatives such as Working for Families.

The research has also enabled us to improve our integrated range of childcare, guidance and education services in response to changing local needs. Unfortunately, the childcare infrastructure remains the biggest obstacle to the progress of individual parents and childcare providers. Our research clearly shows that parents want to move out of poverty, but not at the expense of their children's well-being. They want access to affordable quality childcare, but this is not readily available for all parents. There is very little childcare for parents making transitions from adult literacy and lifelong learning classes to further and higher education. Furthermore, although Working for Families helps some parents to take up work, for example, by subsidising childcare costs for the first few months, childcare in the UK remains the most expensive in Europe.[5] Problems caused by under- and overpayments of childcare tax credits are well documented. As a childcare provider, we experience pressure from funders to increase sustainability by reducing grant dependency by increasing parental fees. Some nurseries which have been driven down this route have only been able to do so by relinquishing their anti-poverty objectives.

Ironically, the welfare to work approach to alleviate poverty, favoured by the UK government and Scottish Executive, has resulted in in-work poverty in the sector which is designed to be the bridge to employment for parents; the hidden losers in childcare are the low-paid members of this predominantly female workforce working in voluntary and private sector nurseries where we are unable to maintain parity with nurseries paying slightly better local authority salaries. As an organisation which supports women to move out of poverty, including in-work poverty, we are painfully aware of the problem of the undervalued childcare profession.

Notes

1   S Innes and G Scott, *Women, Care and Transitions*, Rosemount Lifelong Learning Research Report 1, Centre for Research on Families and Relationships and Scottish Poverty Information Unit, 2003; M Gillespie, G Scott and C Lindsay, *Women, Poverty and Transitions to Work*, Rosemount Lifelong Learning Research Report 2, Scottish Poverty Information Unit, 2003; G Scott, M Gillespie and S Innes, *Breaking Barriers: poverty, childcare and mothers' transitions to work*, Rosemount Learning and Scottish Poverty Information Unit, 2003

2   All quotations in the paper are drawn from the Rosemount research projects – see note 1.

3   M Curran, Presentation at Rosemount Lifelong Learning, 1 September 2003

4   Information on Working for Families has been archived by the Scottish Executive, but can be accessed online at: http://www.scotland.gov.uk/ Topics/People/Social-Inclusion/17414/15075/Q/ViewArchived/On

5   Working Families, *Policy Paper on Childcare*, 2006

Seventeen

Community planning partnerships

Stephen Sinclair

In its broadest sense community planning means 'any process through which a Council [comes] together with other organisations to plan, provide for, or promote the well-being of the communities they serve'.[1] In Scotland, community planning refers to a multi-agency community planning partnership (CPP) – comprising the local authority, key local public service providers, and representatives of the voluntary, community and private sectors – working together at neighbourhood, local authority and regional levels. The 2003 Local Government in Scotland Act, which provides the statutory basis for community planning in Scotland, defines it as a process '... by which the public services provided in the area of the local authority are provided... after consultation... among all the public bodies responsible for providing those services; and with such community bodies and other bodies or persons as is appropriate'.[2] Community planning in Scotland is, therefore, comparable to local strategic partnerships in England, community strategy partnerships in Wales, and local strategy partnerships in Northern Ireland, although there are important differences in the statutory contexts, governance arrangements, and local policy making and delivery systems in each country.

The overarching aims of community planning in Scotland are to:

- improve co-ordination between public agencies in developing and delivering services, particularly in cross-cutting policy areas;
- provide a coherent overarching framework to co-ordinate the proliferation of local partnerships created in recent years;
- enhance community engagement and non-public sector involvement in local policy making.

The key features of community planning developed to achieve these aims are:

- community plans – local strategic visions and corresponding policies jointly developed and shared between partners;
- local authorities maintain responsibility for community leadership but also assume a statutory duty to initiate, facilitate and sustain CPPs;
- a statutory obligation on the part of the main public sector organisations to participate in CPPs – that is, health, police and fire service joint boards, Scottish/Highland and Island Enterprise, and regional transport partnerships;
- a statutory duty upon Scottish Executive ministers to promote and encourage community planning;
- a statutory requirement on CPPs to involve the voluntary sector, business and community representatives in policy making.

The implementation of community planning has been deliberately non-prescriptive, as the Scottish Executive argues that '... what is appropriate will depend on local circumstances'.[3] Inevitably, this has lead to variation in the format and operation of CPPs, and it is necessary to be careful in generalising about overall performance and impact. Although CPPs have wide-ranging local policy and service delivery responsibilities, this chapter focuses on only two of these: area regeneration and community engagement.

Community planning partnerships and regeneration

CPPs are the successors to social inclusion partnerships (SIPs), which were the principal area regeneration initiative in Scotland between 1998 and 2004.[4] As the Poverty Alliance notes, CPPs are '... a key policy mechanism of the Scottish Executive to improve public services, tackle social exclusion and promote regeneration and reduce the democratic deficit through increased community participation and engagement in civic life'.[5] The Scottish Executive's 2002 community regeneration statement outlined the rationale behind integrating SIPs into community planning structures.[6] The intention was to ensure that all community planning partners address regeneration and local deprivation as core activities rather than see these as secondary concerns or the responsibility of specialist agencies. Regeneration policy was to be pursued through agencies' mainstream budgets with less reliance on discrete funding of specific projects. The fourth of the Scottish Executive's six *Closing the Opportunity*

Gap objectives is to '... regenerate the most disadvantaged neighbour-hoods – in order that people living there can take advantage of job oppor-tunities and improve their quality of life'.[7] Local action in pursuit of this objective became the responsibility of CPPs in 2004/05, and to ensure that their policies were linked to the Scottish Executive's national priorities, each CPP was required to prepare a regeneration outcome agreement (ROA) for approval by Communities Scotland and Scottish Executive min-isters. ROAs were required to reflect and demonstrate implementation of the Scottish Executive's five national priorities for community regeneration:

- building strong, safe and attractive communities;
- getting people back into work;
- improving health;
- raising educational attainment;
- engaging young people.[8]

An approved ROA was a condition for assuming responsibility for SIPs and accessing Community Regeneration Fund (CRF) resources. Over the three years to 2008, £318 million has been allocated through the CRF to the 15 per cent most deprived data zones in the 2004 Scottish Index of Multiple Deprivation. The latest regeneration policy statement issued by the Scottish Executive in February 2006 reiterated the 'lead strategic role' of CPPs in regeneration '... through the development and delivery of regeneration outcome agreements'.[9]

The integration of SIPs into CPPs is potentially a double-edged sword. On the one hand, 'mainstreaming' regeneration and social inclu-sion into the priorities of key public sector agencies has been advocated for several years.[10] SIPs themselves were generally in favour of integration into local decision-making structures and hoped that this would facilitate improved co-ordination between regeneration and social inclusion poli-cies, and local education, health, equality, community development and safety agendas.[11] On the other hand, absorbing SIPs and local regenera-tion policy within CPPs may result in these being added to existing organ-isational agendas and lost among the many competing duties which CPPs undertake rather than receiving the priority which specialist regen-eration organisations would accord them. For example, an analysis of community plans found that social inclusion was mentioned as a priority theme in only 14 out of 32, although many more prioritised related activi-ties, such as economic development.[12]

Community planning and community engagement

The five Scottish Executive priorities for community regeneration are underpinned by a sixth cross-cutting priority – effectively engaging communities. The statutory guidance on community planning also states that '… effective and genuine engagement of communities is at the heart of community planning'.[13] This emphasis on public involvement has been welcomed by critics of previous regeneration activities which often left local people as passive bystanders to the process.[14] A Communities Scotland report argued that community planning offered an opportunity to extend community engagement and participatory democracy by involving citizens at the beginning of decision-making processes, developing genuine participation rather than traditional consultation, and employing innovative participation methods.[15] The experience of local strategic partnerships in England shows that the statutory requirement to involve voluntary sector and community representatives reinforces their entitlement to participate in policy making rather than being regarded as peripheral outsiders to be occasionally consulted.[16]

CPPs may therefore offer a means to redress the long-standing imbalance between professional 'experts' and 'non-expert' service users and local people in policy making and debates over regeneration and social inclusion. However, if community planning is to realise this potential, the practical obstacles to ensuring voluntary and community sector involvement must be tackled. The Community Planning Implementation Group's review of progress in implementing community planning noted that a number of CPPs and local authorities have found genuine community engagement '… a challenging part of the process'.[17] The local strategic partnership evaluation concluded that effective community and voluntary sector engagement requires significant changes to the conventional rules of engagement and modification of traditional local public sector organisational cultures and power relationships.[18] Specifically, the voluntary and community sectors require assistance and investment from core partners to enable them to make the most of this opportunity. Communities Scotland has developed voluntary national standards for community engagement[19] and funding through the Community Voices programme[20] to assist this process, and the new Scottish local government Improvement Service also has a role in ensuring CPPs follow best practice in this regard.[21] However, the opportunity presented by community planning also poses challenges to the non-government sector, including poverty activists. To be taken seriously as partners in strategic decision making, they must accept the responsibility that comes with this by looking beyond their familiar core activities and local interests, and not be confrontational in their relations with public agencies.[22] It will be difficult for some community and voluntary sector representatives to reconcile this new role with retaining a distinctive and autonomous voice, and it will undoubtedly be difficult for small organisations with few resources to organise and invest in training to meet this challenge. The Poverty Alliance's Community *Planning Toolkit* offers a starting point which can assist this process.

Conclusions

Community planning in Scotland is a long-term reform which will take several years to show significant results. There is no evidence yet of any distinctive outcomes, nor added value in terms of service users' experiences; analyses completed to date have reported on the implementation processes involved in CP rather than its outputs or impacts.[23] The future development and effects of community planning will also depend in large measure on the impact of the 2004 Local Governance in Scotland Act, which introduces the single transferable vote system, increases the likelihood of coalition administrations, and may encourage many long-serving councillors to retire following the May 2007 local elections.

The more optimistic interpretations of community planning believe that 'Scottish local authorities and their partners have become a national learning network on better governance and participation'.[24] The processes are now in place to deliver on the promise of community planning; what is required now is that commitment to it is sustained over the long term by all those involved in developing and delivering local public services.

Notes

1   Community Planning Working Group, *Report of the Community Planning Working Group*, The Scottish Office/COSLA, 1998, p5
2   Local Government in Scotland Act 2003, Part 2, para 15(1), available online at: http://www.opsi.gov.uk/legislation/scotland/acts2003/30001
3   See the Scottish Executive Community Planning website at: http://www.scotland.gov.uk/Topics/Government/local-government/CP/CP
4   G Mooney, 'Local Areas and Regeneration', in U Brown and others (eds), *Poverty in Scotland 2002*, Child Poverty Action Group, 2002, pp108-112
5   Poverty Alliance, *Community Planning Toolkit*, 2005, p8, available online at: http://www.povertyalliance.org/html/resources/publications/commToolkit.pdf

6 Scottish Executive, *Better Communities in Scotland: closing the gap*, 2002, available online at: http://www.scotland.gov.uk/library5/social/bcis-00.asp

7 Scottish Executive, *Closing the Opportunity Gap*, available online at: http://www.scotland.gov.uk/Topics/People/Social-Inclusion/17415/opportunity

8 Communities Scotland, *Community Regeneration Fund: guidance on regeneration outcome agreements*, Scottish Executive, 2004, p4

9 Scottish Executive, *People and Place: regeneration policy statement*, 2006, available online at: http://www.scotland.gov.uk/Publications/2006/02/2 4092959/10

10 C Lipman, 'In Search of the Mainstream', *New Start*, 24 May 2002, p1

11 M Carley, *Implementing Community Planning: building for the future of local governance*, Communities Scotland, 2004, p28

12 P Spicker, *Community Planning in Scotland*, Centre for Public Policy and Management Working Paper 4, Robert Gordon University, 2004, available online at: http://www2.rgu.ac.uk/publicpolicy/cppm/complan.pdf

13 Scottish Executive, *The Local Government in Scotland Act 2003: community planning: statutory guidance*, 2004, p7, para 5.1

14 Sustainable Development Commission, *Mainstreaming Sustainable Regeneration: a call to action*, 2003

15 See note 11, pvii

16 M Taylor, 'Communities in Partnership: developing a strategic voice', *Social Policy and Society*, 2006, Vol 5.2, p272

17 Community Planning Implementation Group, *Making a Difference: community planning a year on*, 2004, p5

18 Office of the Deputy Prime Minister, *National Evaluation of Local Strategic Partnerships: formative evaluation and action research programme 2002–2005*, 2006

19 Communities Scotland, *National Standards for Community Engagement*, 2006, available online at: http://www.communitiesscotland.gov.uk/stellent/groups/ public/documents/webpages/cs_010771.hcsp#TopOfPage

20 Communities Scotland, *Community Voices Programme*, available online at: http://www.communitiesscotland.gov.uk/stellent/groups/public/documents/web pages/cs_011085.hcsp#TopOfPage

21 The Improvement Service is a private company established jointly between the Scottish Executive, the Confederation of Scottish Local Authorities and the Society of Local Authority Chief Executives to promote best practice in local government in Scotland. See http://www.improvementservice.org.uk/index.php

22 See note 16, p275

23 Audit Scotland, *Community Planning: an initial review*, 2006

24 See note 11, pv

Eighteen
Rural poverty
John H McKendrick

What is the problem?

Rural poverty and the quality of rural life are issues of concern in contemporary Scotland. Rural Scotland is not always cast in a favourable light when compared to urban Scotland: people have to travel further to access essential services; households spend more on motor fuel; food is significantly more expensive; there is more dissatisfaction with local shops, local leisure facilities and public transport; average pay is lower; and employment is more seasonal.[1] Most importantly, there is poverty in rural Scotland. Indeed, the proportion of people living in poverty in rural Scotland is comparable to the proportion of people living in poverty in urban Scotland (Table 4.12). The Scottish Executive is sensitive to these challenges facing rural Scotland, has introduced policies and devised plans to tackle problems and enhance life in rural Scotland, and has a ministerial portfolio with primary responsibility for rural Scotland.[2]

One of the key problems of rural poverty in Scotland is that it is less visible than Scotland's urban poverty.

There are five inter-related reasons why Scotland's rural poverty is hidden. First, rural poverty lacks credibility when our predominant understanding of the countryside is that it is a place of beauty and one in which we can escape the problems and pressures of our urban lives. Second, independence and self-sufficiency are more highly valued in rural areas making it more likely that unmet need is unknown need to the policy maker. This culture of self-reliance leads to a paradox of invisibility as, alongside the invisibility of poverty to external service providers, the close-knit nature of small communities makes it more likely that these unmet needs will be known within the community. Third, the absence, inaccessibility and costs of accessing key services result in lower service uptake, with the further consequence that problems may not be brought to the attention of service providers. Fourth, rural poverty is dispersed and is more easily hidden from view than that of inner-city neighbourhoods and multiply deprived housing estates on the outskirts of our urban areas where we have come to expect to find poverty. Finally, for too long there has been systematic urban bias in how we collect information on poverty and on how we implement anti-poverty strategies. Our concerns to tackle the most visible expressions of poverty in the largest concentrations, and our concern to establish national measures of poverty, have inadvertently led to an urbanisation of concern with poverty in Scotland.

What is being done?

The deeply entrenched practices which marginalise 'the rural' in poverty debates in Scotland are now being challenged. In addition to the raft of national (urban and rural) initiatives that are being initiated to tackle poverty in Scotland, there are four developments that suggest that the problem of rural poverty has been recognised and is being addressed.

First, since its inception the Scottish Executive has organised its business to give focus to rural issues. A Minister for Rural Affairs was appointed in 1999 and Scottish Executive rural policy was co-ordinated first by a Ministerial Committee on Rural Development, and then by a Cabinet Sub-Committee on Rural Development. The current partnership agreement, commits the Executive to '…ensure that rural and remote communities have their distinct needs reflected across the range of government policy and initiatives'.[3]

Second, the Executive has delivered in progressing rural debate. Its strategy for rural policy was set out in 2000 with the publication of *Rural Scotland: a new approach* and progress reports were published in 2003 and 2004.[4] It is currently consulting on its *Rural Development Programme for Scotland 2007–2013*.[5]

Third, *Closing the Opportunity Gap*, the Scottish Executive's social justice strategy, comprises a specific target to tackle the problem of rural service delivery.[6] Target H seeks to '…by 2008, improve service delivery in rural areas so that agreed improvements in accessibility and quality are achieved for key services in remote and disadvantaged communities'. In December 2005, 22 rural service priority areas were allocated £100,000 to develop new projects. More generally, each of the other nine targets is required to consider the rural dimension.

Finally, Scottish Executive-led approaches to understanding and measuring poverty and social exclusion have shown sensitivity to the rural dimension. In 2001 it published *Poverty and Social Exclusion in Rural Scotland*, a report by the Scottish Executive-convened Rural Poverty and Inclusion Working Group.[7] Furthermore, one of the seven dimensions of the *Scottish Index of Multiple Deprivation* is a measure of geographical access to services, which acknowledges the importance of poverty of access in rural Scotland.[8]

What is left to do?

It is the pace of change and intensity of effort – rather than the direction of change – that is the most pressing issue in the quest to tackle rural poverty in Scotland. More of the same is needed more quickly. In giving focus to this challenge, this chapter concludes with five recommendations.

First, rural anti-poverty activity must be taken more seriously in the fight against poverty in Scotland. The Scottish Executive is championing action in priority areas (transport, access to key services, using communications and information technology to tackle network poverty [the connections which provide social support and information on opportunities]. Most significantly, the Executive is using a model of implementation that is fit-for-purpose (communities defining their own priorities), thereby acknowledging the diversity of rural Scotland. However, inadvertently, this implies that it cannot be assumed that successful pilots can be rolled out unproblematically across rural Scotland. Further support and careful judgement will be needed if the benefits of pilot schemes are to be realised across rural Scotland. Furthermore, rather than (as currently) portraying the focus and approach to anti-poverty strategy in rural areas as a sensitive adaptation to rural circumstances, there is merit in recasting its small-scale, people-centred, bottom-up approach as an alternative to the grand schemes of urban Scotland that have consistently failed to make inroads into urban poverty. The character of the anti-poverty work undertaken in rural areas should be less of a sideshow and more of a vanguard.

Second, low pay in rural Scotland must be challenged and, albeit difficult for the Executive to address, cannot be sidelined or ignored.

Third, *Closing the Opportunity Gap* has to demonstrate that the programme to tackle rural poverty in Scotland extends beyond Target H and service delivery. The reality is that just as Target H is directed only at rural areas, other targets imply action which is focused mainly on urban areas (for example, Target A, which aims to reduce the number of work-less people dependent on social security benefits in five urban local authorities). More generally, the *Closing the Opportunity Gap* focus on reducing poverty may inadvertently lead to a concentration of effort on where most gain can be made most quickly – in urban Scotland.

Fourth, we need to show statistical sophistication when interpreting the objective facts of poverty in Scotland and we need to be aware of the different experiences of living in poverty in different parts of Scotland. The key message must be that poverty is as prevalent in rural Scotland as it is in urban Scotland. Likewise, research must seek to understand and then to tackle the problems associated with the experience of living in poverty outside multiply deprived areas.

Finally, we need a measure of rural deprivation. Of course, it is essential that we have national measures – such as the Department for Work and Pensions' new child poverty measure,[9] or the Scottish Executive's Scottish Index of Multiple Deprivation[10] – that allow us to con-trast urban and rural experiences. However, these national measures must focus on issues of key importance to the whole nation. There is a strong case for predominantly rural local authorities in Scotland to work together to introduce a measure of rural poverty and deprivation, which would pro-vide insight into the particularities of rural poverty in Scotland, thereby complementing the work of the Scottish Executive.

Notes

1　T Edwards, Rural Development, *SPICe Briefing 05/10*, The SPICe, 2005; End Child Poverty, NCH and Forum for Rural Children and Young People, *Rural Child Poverty Briefing Paper*, 2003; Scottish Executive, *Social Focus on Urban Rural Scotland 2003*, 2003, available online at: http://www.scotland.gov.uk/Publications/2003/05/17207/22173; Scottish Executive, *Social Focus on Deprived Areas 2005*, 2005, available online at: http://www.scotland.gov.uk/Publications/2005/09/2792129/21311

2　Scottish Executive, *Rural Development Programme for Scotland 2007–2013*, 2006, available online at: http://www.scotland.gov.uk/Publications/2006/02/08132503/0

3　On the other hand, the co-ordinating committees no longer meet, the holistic focus on 'rural affairs' was superceded in 2003 with a narrower focus on 'rural development and environment', and there is no formal policy of mainstreaming rural issues across Executive policy.

4　Scottish Executive, *Rural Scotland: a new approach*, 2000, available online at: http://www.scotland.gov.uk/library2/doc15/rsna-00.asp; Scottish Executive,

Annual Rural Report 2003, 2003; Scottish Executive, *Annual Rural Report 2004*, 2004

5 See note 2

6 Scottish Executive, *Closing the Opportunity Gap, Target H*, 2006, available online at: http://www.scotland.gov.uk/Topics/People/Social-Inclusion/17415/CtOG-targets/CtOG-target-h

7 Rural Poverty and Inclusion Working Group, *Poverty and Social Exclusion in Rural Scotland*, Scottish Executive, 2006, available online at: http://www.scotland.gov.uk/library3/society/pser-00.asp

8 Scottish Executive, *Scottish Index of Multiple Deprivation 2006*, 2006, available online at: http://www.scotland.gov.uk/News/Releases/2006/10/17104536

9 Department for Work and Pensions, *Measuring Child Poverty*, Department for Work and Pensions, 2003, available online at: www.dwp.gov.uk/ofa/related/final_conclusions.pdf

10 See note 8

Section Four
Conclusions

Nineteen
Conclusions
Gerry Mooney

From the evidence provided throughout this book it is clear that great strides have been made in producing meaningful data at a Scottish level that informs our understanding of the extent and patterns of poverty across Scotland today. We have come a considerable way since the author of the first book in this series complained about the absence of useful Scottish poverty data. Although this represents a change from the past, there are also important continuities. The diverse range of new sources and types of information serve to remind us once again that poverty is deeply entrenched within Scottish society. Important inroads have been made by governments across the UK in addressing poverty for certain sections of the population, for example children. For other groups, such as childless adults, much remains to be done.

The task that falls to this final chapter is to pull together some of the main themes and issues that emerge from the previous sections of this book, and also to offer some tentative conclusions through which we raise important questions that matter to all of those who are concerned with poverty in contemporary Scotland and how it is to be effectively tackled.

Themes and issues

In the previous edition of *Poverty in Scotland* in 2002 we acknowledged that the current government, unlike its predecessor, could not be accused of 'doing nothing' about poverty. It is to the Scottish Executive's and UK Government's credit that they have continued in similar vein since the elections in 2003 and 2005. However, government policies and statements also tell us a great deal about the definition and understanding of poverty that is being used when developing policy. From the analysis provided throughout this book it is clear that poverty is to be understood primarily as resulting from exclusion from paid employment. It is this, above all else, which drives government anti-poverty policy today.

It is evident from the essays in Section Three that the current Government has sought to develop policies across the range of areas that relate most directly to poverty. Child poverty is one area that has been frequently earmarked for particular attention, and has been an area where there has been real improvement, with a notable reduction in child poverty rates in Scotland in recent years. Even so, with almost one in four children still living in poverty today, this remains unacceptably high – and almost double the rate of 1979. This chimes with another theme that emerges from Section Three – that while there have been some improvements in recent years, certainly when compared with the 1980s and 1990s (at least in relation to poverty rates, if not in terms of income and wealth inequalities), we have not as yet reduced the extent and depth of relative poverty to levels that were experienced in the 1960s and 1970s – which even then were regarded as being too high.

Returning to a point made in Section One, this is a book that is concerned with poverty in many different forms. However, it is not feasible to ignore wider social and economic inequalities and several of the contributions to Section Three emphasise that poverty will not be effectively addressed until income poverty is tackled, in part through the provision of increased cash benefits and better public services which remain free at the point of delivery. This is linked to other debates about the nature of welfare provision. Here, the main argument revolves around the *universal* provision of benefits and services or, as favoured by successive governments, more *selective*, means-tested and targeted approaches to social welfare. It could be argued that such a dichotomy is false, given that many of the services that the post-war welfare state has provided have never been universal. The concern that many people have is that the *principle* of universalism is being increasingly undermined by the use of means-testing to target benefits and services. This makes for a welfare system that is less effective in preventing and protecting all citizens from poverty.

Employment, citizenship and social justice

Closing the Opportunity Gap, which at the time of writing is the key plank in the Scottish Executive's anti-poverty social policy, has rightly featured in a number of the different chapters in this collection. As we noted in

Section One, it is a development of the Scottish Executive's original social justice strategy and one of the underlying themes that emerges from the discussions offered in Sections Two and Three. It also raises wider issues and questions about the nature of citizenship and the role of employment in early twenty-first century Scotland. How is equal citizenship to be achieved? How is equality to be attained? What is the role of paid employment as a means of tackling poverty and as a route to inclusion and citizenship? For many commentators, the *Closing the Opportunity Gap* approach does not go nearly far enough in providing answers to these questions. It ignores the large gap between rich and poor, a point to which we return below; through focusing on work as the route to personal prosperity it marginalises important questions of in-work poverty and for many more workers across Scotland it neglects crucial issues of job insecurity, casualisation, labour market 'churning' (that is regular periods of work interspersed with periodic unemployment) – and, of course, of adequate pension provision in old age. Others have noted that the continuing questions of adequate and affordable childcare have yet to be adequately addressed (and indeed some would argue that the Scotland-wide strike in 2004 of local authority-employed nursery nurses is a reflection of a wider and deeper devaluing of childcare across Scottish and UK society today).

Scotland is undergoing profound social and economic change. Some changes should be welcomed as being beneficial to all of Scottish society, for example, the ban on smoking in public places introduced in early 2006. But in other ways, for many more people across Scotland – asylum seekers, lone mothers and fathers, childless couples, many pensioners and for those in poor-quality and low-paid employment – Scotland remains an insecure and uncertain place. Tackling such insecurity and uncertainty is not something that can be done through one policy measure – but it is an important element of an effective attack on poverty. What we can be sure of is that paid employment, although central to tackling poverty, does not provide security for many of the groups of citizens mentioned above. Nor will it provide a route to inclusion and social justice for many of those who experience poverty in Scotland at the moment. We must begin to find other ways to an inclusive society, ways that do not rely solely on access to the labour market.

Making poverty history?

One of the most significant stories of poverty in Scotland in recent years revolves around the huge Making Poverty History demonstration in Edinburgh in July 2005. Taking place against the backdrop of the G8 Summit at Gleneagles Hotel, hundreds of thousands of campaigners reminded us that there can be an alternative to a world – and a Scotland – scourged by poverty and want. As Richard Wilkinson has ably demonstrated in his book *The Impact of Inequality*:[1]

> What matters in the developed world today is the social environment: it is only by improving the quality of social relations that we can make further improvements in the real quality of our lives. Fortunately, the quality of the social environment is not simply a matter for individual wishful thinking or individual commitment to higher moral standards: it is instead built on material foundations. Practical policies affecting how we run the economy and how the organisations we work in function provide powerful policy handles with which to influence the nature of social life.

Turning to the Scottish Parliament elections taking place this year – and beyond to the third term of the re-convened Scottish Parliament, we made the point at the outset that this is a book concerned primarily with poverty and social exclusion. However, it is clear that the continuing prevalence of poverty in Scotland in the early twenty-first century is related in different ways to the growing inequalities in income and wealth that are such a notable feature of both the UK and Scotland in recent decades. Here, we are reminded again of the point made by a number of the contributors to Section Three that low income and income poverty remain to be addressed in an effective and comprehensive way. However, while the Government has been 'busy' at the 'lower end' of the social spectrum in developing policies to address poverty and social exclusion, it has been reluctant to do anything that would challenge the major sources of inequality in society (and indeed many critics argue that the dominant economic and social policies it has pursued have worked to increase the gulf between rich and poor). Adrian Sinfield has argued that we need to 'move upstream' in our analysis and comprehension of poverty. *Upstream* policies focus on the root causes of disadvantages and inequalities in society whereas *downstream* strategies seek to manage and ameliorate the consequences of these.[2] In many ways this is a call for more preventive strategies. Removing people from poverty, for instance from pensioner poverty, fuel poverty or child poverty, must remain an important element of policy making, but more attention needs to be given to how we prevent people from falling into poverty in the first place. For the present UK Government this is predominantly and increasingly understood in individ-ualised terms, in terms of individual failures – such as the failure to engage in paid work or to fulfil parental or familial responsibilities. This frequently gives rise to a stigmatising and demonising way of thinking about poor people that can only undermine the fight against poverty and social exclu-sion in all its forms. Unfortunately, such thinking is not being marginalised but appears to be becoming more and more significant in government thinking. Across the UK in recent years there has been an emerging and increasing emphasis by governments on 'the problems caused' by a range of socially disadvantaged groups, most recently shown in the UK Government's ten-year action plan on social exclusion.[3] Talk of anti-social behaviour, poor parenting, individual worklessness, truancy and so on all contribute to ways of thinking that tend to see different forms of behaviour modification and reshaping as the key policies that should be pursued. This carries important consequences for the understanding of poverty, social disadvantage and inequality in Scotland and the UK today. In par-ticular, it helps to develop and reinforce a 'residualised' view of poverty which regards poverty, and in particular income poverty, as marginal to the 'main' social problems affecting society. It also suggests that poverty has been largely 'fixed', except among a minority and recalcitrant group largely 'untouched' as yet by policies.

Emerging ideas among politicians and policy makers speak of those individuals and communities that are either underperforming or otherwise not contributing to the overall 'social good'. Such people and places are seen as an increasing threat to social cohesion and to social solidarity. In all of this, it is an easy task to identify historic concerns with the 'disrep-utable poor' and more recently with 'the underclass'. We hope that this book will help to promote an understanding of poverty, which reinforces approaches to anti-poverty strategy that focus on underlying structural causes rather than on individual behaviours.

A concern with welfare to work remains central to anti-poverty pol-icy in Scotland, as in the rest of the UK. Tackling poverty in turn is seen as essential to the successful regeneration and enhanced competitiveness of the Scottish economy and to the vision of a *Smart, Successful Scotland* as heralded by Scottish ministers.[4] First Minister Jack McConnell, addressing the Scottish Parliament on 6 September 2006, stated that the

Scottish Executive 'remain resolved to abolishing child poverty by 2020'. We welcome the re-emphasis on attacking poverty but remain concerned that over-focusing on paid work, on efficient labour markets and on individual failure will undermine such an objective. To have any real prospect of delivering on earlier commitments to create a socially just Scotland 'where everybody matters', it is vital that all Scottish policy makers realise that social policy, and particularly anti-poverty policy, is not a mere adjunct to economic policy.

Notes

1 RG Wilkinson, *The Impact of Inequality*, Routledge, 2005, pp314–15
2 A Sinfield, 'Upstream Thinking', in *Policy World*, Social Policy Association Newsletter, Autumn 2004, p10
3 Cabinet Office, *Reaching Out: an action plan on social exclusion, 2006*, available online at: http://www.cabinetoffice.gov.uk/social_exclusion_task_force/reaching_out/reaching_out.asp
4 Scottish Executive, *Smart, Successful Scotland*, 2001

Appendix One
Policy diary
Peter Kelly

Date	Westminster/ Scotland	Legislation	Area of interest covered	Website
2003	Scotland	Education (School Meals) (Scotland) Act	• Amendment to Education (Scotland) Act 1980 to ensure continued entitlement to free school meals for people claiming income-based jobseeker's allowance or income support following the introduction of tax credits	http://www.opsi. gov.uk/legislation/ scotland/acts2003/ 20030018.htm
2003	Westminster	Income Tax (Earnings and Pensions) Act	• Earnings/incomes • Tax on earnings/ incomes • Taxable benefits	http://www.opsi.gov. uk/acts/acts2003/ 20030001.htm
2003	Westminster	National Minimum Wage (Enforcement Notices) Act	• Enabling enforcements under Minimum Wage Act 1999	http://www.opsi.gov. uk/acts/acts2003/ 20030008.htm
2004	Scotland	Antisocial Behaviour etc (Scotland) Act	• Strategies for anti- social behaviour • Extension of anti-social behaviour orders to 12–15-year-olds • Increased powers of dispersal and closure of premises	http://www.opsi.gov. uk/legislation/ scotland/acts2004/ 20040008.htm
2004	Westminster	Asylum and Immigration (Treatment of Claimants, etc) Act 2004	• Immigration • Employment rights for asylum seekers • Welfare benefits for asylum seekers	http://www.opsi.gov. uk/acts/acts2004/ 20040019.htm

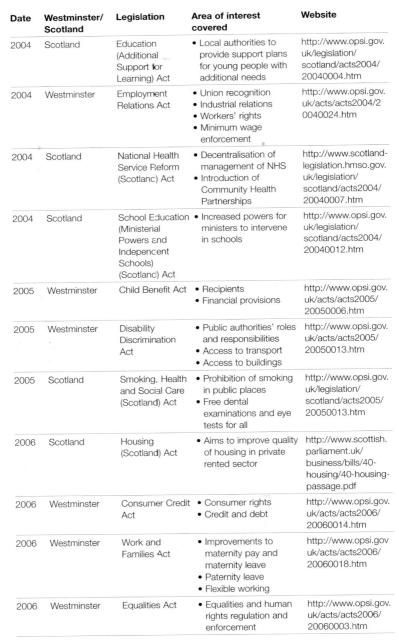

Date	Westminster/ Scotland	Legislation	Area of interest covered	Website
2004	Scotland	Education (Additional Support for Learning) Act	• Local authorities to provide support plans for young people with additional needs	http://www.opsi.gov. uk/legislation/ scotland/acts2004/ 20040004.htm
2004	Westminster	Employment Relations Act	• Union recognition • Industrial relations • Workers' rights • Minimum wage enforcement	http://www.opsi.gov. uk/acts/acts2004/2 0040024.htm
2004	Scotland	National Health Service Reform (Scotland) Act	• Decentralisation of management of NHS • Introduction of Community Health Partnerships	http://www.scotland-legislation.hmso.gov. uk/legislation/ scotland/acts2004/ 20040007.htm
2004	Scotland	School Education (Ministerial Powers and Independent Schools) (Scotland) Act	• Increased powers for ministers to intervene in schools	http://www.opsi.gov. uk/legislation/ scotland/acts2004/ 20040012.htm
2005	Westminster	Child Benefit Act	• Recipients • Financial provisions	http://www.opsi.gov. uk/acts/acts2005/ 20050006.htm
2005	Westminster	Disability Discrimination Act	• Public authorities' roles and responsibilities • Access to transport • Access to buildings	http://www.opsi.gov. uk/acts/acts2005/ 20050013.htm
2005	Scotland	Smoking, Health and Social Care (Scotland) Act	• Prohibition of smoking in public places • Free dental examinations and eye tests for all	http://www.opsi.gov. uk/legislation/ scotland/acts2005/ 20050013.htm
2006	Scotland	Housing (Scotland) Act	• Aims to improve quality of housing in private rented sector	http://www.scottish. parliament.uk/ business/bills/40-housing/40-housing-passage.pdf
2006	Westminster	Consumer Credit Act	• Consumer rights • Credit and debt	http://www.opsi.gov. uk/acts/acts2006/ 20060014.htm
2006	Westminster	Work and Families Act	• Improvements to maternity pay and maternity leave • Paternity leave • Flexible working	http://www.opsi.gov uk/acts/acts2006/ 20060018.htm
2006	Westminster	Equalities Act	• Equalities and human rights regulation and enforcement	http://www.opsi.gov. uk/acts/acts2006/ 20060003.htm

Appendix Two

Poverty statistics for Scotland: what we have and what we now need

John H McKendrick

It is an appropriate moment to take stock of the information now available on poverty in Scotland; post-devolution developments – such as several key Great Britain (GB)/UK surveys increasing the number of people surveyed in Scotland and the introduction of new Scotland-wide surveys – are now firmly established. However, it is also an opportune moment to assess the adequacy of poverty data which is now available; for example, is there sufficient data for the Scottish Executive to evaluate *Closing the Opportunity Gap*,[1] its flagship anti-poverty programme, and what implications would follow if the Scottish Household Survey changed from a regular survey schedule to a survey design comprising core and rotating modules?[2]

It is argued that Scotland needs a 'Poverty and Social Inclusion' module in the Scottish Household Survey and that a toolkit should be made publicly available to facilitate locality and sub-group studies of poverty in Scotland by third party interest groups.

The starting point for this appendix is a Scottish Poverty Information Unit (SPIU) discussion paper of 1998, which reviewed poverty data availability in Scotland prior to devolution and the introduction of the Scottish Household Survey in 1999. Subsequent changes in policy, data availability and research practice are outlined, before a critical appraisal of the current situation is offered. A recommendation for a 'Poverty and Social Inclusion' module in the Scottish Household Survey follows from the conclusion that more information is needed on poverty in Scotland.

Information for a change

In 1988, SPIU examined 'the need for improved information on poverty to aid effective anti-poverty work within the context of a devolved Scotland'.[3] Set against the context of a Scotland in which levels of poverty increased for almost two decades and for which poverty information was often extrapolated from GB/UK data, the paper presented the 'case for more adequate information on Scotland... with the prospect of a Scottish Parliament with powers to fight against poverty'.[4] It welcomed the prospect of the Scottish Household Survey, particularly as it would allow disaggregation of data to local authority level and given that social exclusion was understood to be one of the subject areas for development.

Although not concluding with firm recommendations, SPIU's paper specified the components of a poverty assessment strategy, introduced the main approaches to poverty measurement and presented a 'Scottish dimension', which outlined the limitations of different approaches to measuring poverty in Scotland. SPIU identified the fact that data were frequently only available at the level of GB/UK and suggested that behavioural patterns, population composition, basic needs derived from a harsher climatic environment and the cost of (rural) living set Scotland apart from the rest of the UK. These differences rendered problematic straightforward inference of poverty in Scotland from GB/UK data. These problems are exacerbated for local authorities within Scotland in the absence of adequate small area-level data. The lack of sufficiently detailed data on expenditure patterns in Scotland and the dearth of longitudinal data were identified as particular limitations.

Almost ten years on, and Scotland still does not yet have adequate data to understand, appraise and tackle poverty in Scotland. Almost ten years on, and the Scottish Household Survey still holds the most promise for addressing our poverty data deficiencies. However, significant progress has been made since SPIU's discussion paper, and before appraisals and recommendations are proposed, it is necessary to summarise change since the millennium.

Scotland and poverty since the millennium

The landscape of Scottish poverty has changed markedly in a short space of time. Poverty in Scotland is falling,[5] the UK Government has given a firm commitment to eradicate child poverty within a generation (also endorsed by the Scottish Executive), and facilitating social inclusion has moved up the political agenda in Scotland, first through the social justice milestones and, more recently, with the *Closing the Opportunity Gap* programme.

Allied to these political changes, have been a series of developments which have improved data availability in Scotland. The introduction of the Scottish Household Survey in 1999 was a significant potential gain, with its ability to contribute to an understanding of life in each of Scotland's 32 local authorities over its two-year survey cycle, as was the Scottish-booster to the sample of the *British Household Panel Survey*.[6] Most significantly, improved geographical coverage in Scotland since April 2001 with the inclusion of sampling in the Highlands and Islands, means that the *Family Resources Survey* now provides more robust Scottish-level data.[7] This is particularly important as this is the resource used by the Department for Work and Pensions to measure the level of child poverty.[8]

Data is now more readily available and accessible with user-friendly interfaces on survey websites and the online publication of annual reports, thematic reports and briefing papers. As Table A1 demonstrates, a wealth of poverty, and particularly social inclusion, data can be derived from a number of national surveys.

Yet despite these welcome developments, deficiencies persist. The *Scottish Household Survey* and Scottish booster of the *British Household Panel Survey* have not fully realised their potential as tools to inform understanding of poverty and social inclusion. Furthermore, the wider trend in social research toward inclusive, active and participative research involving, if not led by, the subjects of research,[9] is not being embraced by government in the study of poverty. Finally, we do not have sufficient data to compare Scotland in its wider European context using the set of 18 Laeken social exclusion indicators, which the European Union (EU) has adopted as an EU-wide suite of poverty measures.[10]

What we have

Official government measures of poverty in Scotland are drawn from the annual survey of 2,000 households in Scotland, as part of the Great Britain-wide *Family Resources Survey*. Two key measures are derived from this source. First, measures of absolute and relative low-income poverty are derived from the *Households Below Average Income* (HBAI)

Table A1:
Key national data sources on poverty in Scotland

Title	Poverty data	Design	Sample
Scottish Household Survey	Household income, credit and debt. More generally, information relevant to devolved decision making.	Continuous cross-sectional survey since 1999.	31,000 household interviews every two years. Nationally representative sample every three months, large local authority sample annually and small local authority sample every two years.
Scottish Household Panel Survey	Core question on income. Has included questions on wealth and debt. Also general well-being and family circumstances.	Longitudinal, annual survey since 1991.	Initial GB sample of 5,000 households and 10,000 individual adults. Since 1999, boosted sample in Scotland; now 1,500 cohort members in Scotland.
Scottish House Condition Survey	Household income and neighbourhood environment.	Continuous survey since 2003. Longitudinal component (dwellings) in surveys of 1991, 1996 and 2002.	
British Birth Cohort Study	General well-being and family circumstances.	Longitudinal. Follow-up on sample born in 1970 (1970, 1975, 1980, 1986, 1996, 1999).	Initial UK sample of 16,135. In 1999, around 1,000 cohort members in Scotland were interviewed.
National Child Development Study	General well-being and family circumstances.	Longitudinal. Follow-up on sample born in 1958 (1958, 1965, 1969, 1974, 1978, 1981, 1991, 1999).	Initial UK sample of 17,414. In 1999, around 1,000 cohort members in Scotland were interviewed.
ESRC Millennium Cohort Study	General well-being and family circumstances. Poverty and wealth is identified as a long-term focus.	Longitudinal (2000/01).	Initial UK sample of 15,000. Initial sample boosted in Scotland to 2,500.

Title	Poverty data	Design	Sample
Survey of Low Income Families	Life in low-income families. Focus on work incentives and family welfare.	Longitudinal, annual since 1999.	Initial UK sample of 5,397 families. Initial sample of around 400 in Scotland.
West of Scotland 20-07 Study	Health inequalities and place.	Longitudinal, follow-up on sample of 15-, 35- and 55-year olds in 1987 (six waves in total).	3,000 in West of Scotland regional sample and 1,800 in two small areas in Glasgow.
Labour Force Survey	Income. More generally, on employment and unemployment.	Continuous survey. Quarterly since 1992 (annually 1984–1991 and bi-annually 1973–1983).	UK sample of 120,000 adults in 60,000 households per year. 1,200 households interviewed in Scotland every quarter. Annual figures for local authorities and LECs in Scotland.
Family Resources Survey	Household income. Source of HBAI data. More generally, on family expenditure.	Continuous survey, since 1993.	GB sample of 26,000 households per year. 2,000 households interviewed in Scotland every year. Since 2001 includes the Highlands and Islands.
Millennium Poverty and Social Exclusion Survey	Living standards and poverty. Also general well-being.	Cross-sectional survey, 1983, 1990 and 1999.	GB sample of 1,534 individuals in 1999. 202 individuals interviewed in Scotland.
Scottish Index of Multiple Deprivation 2006	Income deprivation. Six other domains of deprivation and overall (multiple) deprivation for small areas in Scotland (data zones).	Utilises most recent data prior to 2006.	6,505 data zones in Scotland.

data. The level and incidence of poverty, at different thresholds, is reported for children, adults of working age and pensioners. Second, the *Family Resources Survey* presents data on material deprivation for adults and children. These data, first collected in 2004, comprise 11 measures of adult deprivation and nine measures of child deprivation. The drive to promote social inclusion has also involved the Scottish Executive monitoring progress annually for its set of key indicators – the 30 social justice milestones from 1999 to 2004 and the ten *Closing the Opportunity Gap* targets from 2004.

Collectively, and as Section Two of this book has demonstrated, these wide-ranging national resources deliver a robust national portrait of poverty in Scotland. However, this is also a limitation. First, the national scale at which this data is presented promotes an understanding that the incidence and experience of poverty is uniform across Scotland. Second, the size and composition of the *Family Resources Survey* sample in Scotland does not allow for detailed analysis of the poverty of many key sub-groups (for instance, black and minority ethnic communities, asylum seekers and carers).[11]

What we now need

Scotland needs more detailed information on the distribution of poverty within Scotland. The proposed solution to this problem comprises two parts.

First, the full potential of the Scottish Household Survey should be realised. This has failed to deliver as a tool for examining poverty and social inclusion in Scotland, particularly given the importance of social inclusion/closing opportunity gaps to the agenda of the Scottish Executive and the overarching goal of the Scottish Household Survey to provide information to inform government decision-making in Scotland. Four principles should guide the design.

- The Scottish Household Survey should replicate those indicators used by the UK government to measure child poverty in Great Britain. These indicators should be an integral part of the core Scottish Household Survey schedule. This would enable each local authority in Scotland to compare itself against Great Britain and Scotland trends.
- The routine analysis of the proposed questions for the core of the

Scottish Household Survey should be extended beyond the analysis of child poverty to include the broader analysis recommended in the Laeken indicators. This would enable Scotland (and each local authority therein) to compare itself against UK and European trends.

- Scotland-wide debate with third party interest groups should be undertaken to identify key dimensions of poverty in Scotland that are not included in the official EU and UK definitions of poverty. Indicators for these measures should be devised and incorporated in the Scottish Household Survey schedule.
- Cognisance of wider debates in poverty measurement should be taken, with a view to piloting key measures of poverty that are being proposed by experts in Scotland and beyond. The Scottish Household Survey could become a key resource for poverty measurement in Scotland and beyond as the results for new measures could be compared to the findings of the established measures at the core of the Survey schedule.

There are three issues to consider in response to this proposal. First, the additional costs involved in improving the income measure in the Scottish Household Survey may be a deterrent. Significantly, this issue has been considered in recent reports commissioned by the Scottish Executive and Communities Scotland and, notwithstanding the need to improve data collection and manipulation (imputation) practices, the experts conclude that this is not an insurmountable problem.[12] Second, any expansion in the survey schedule of the coverage of income would imply a reduction in the coverage of other themes. This could be problematic given the independent Scottish Household Survey review considered that the schedule was generating information that was relevant and was being used to address devolved matters.[13] However, overcoming social inclusion and tackling poverty is purported to lie at the heart of the agenda of the Scottish Executive and UK Government. Time must be found to incorporate more robust measures of poverty and social inclusion in the Scottish Household Survey schedule if it is to achieve its goal of being a resource that attends to the needs of a devolved Scottish Parliament. Third, in light of the difficulties faced in incorporating fit-for-purpose poverty and social inclusion questions in the Survey, it might be argued that its presentation as a rotating module would suffice. This would be adequate, providing that its modular design allowed for analysis at local authority level. At present, this is not possible, as the smaller local authorities only obtain a robust sample on completion of the full two-year Survey cycle.

Table A2:

Draft schedule for a Poverty and Social Exclusion module in the Scottish Household Survey

Measure	Base	Question	Response	External benchmark
Adult material deprivation	You and family	• Keep home adequately warm. • Two pairs of all weather shoes for each adult. • Enough money to keep home in decent state of repair. • Holiday away from home for one week a year, not staying with relatives. • Replace any worn out furniture. • Small amount of money each week to spend on self, not family. • Regular savings (£10/month) for rainy days/retirement. • Insurance of dwelling contents. • Have friends or family for drink or mea at least once per month. • Hobby or leisure pursuit. • Replace or repair broken electrical goods.	1. Yes 2. No, but would like 3. No, but do not want/ need	UK Government child poverty measure of material deprivation
Adult material deprivation	You and family	[selective additional questions following consultation with third party interest groups]		None
Child material deprivation	Each child	• Holiday away from home for one week a year, with family. • Swimming, at least monthly. • Hobby or leisure pursuit. • Friends for snack or tea at least once per fortnight. • Own bedroom for every child over 10 of different sex. • Leisure equipment. • Celebrations on special occasions. • Play/nursery/toddler group, weekly for children of pre-school age. • School trip, termly, for children of school age.	1. Yes 2. No, but they would like 3. No, but they do not want/need	UK Government child poverty measure of material deprivation

Child material deprivation	Each child	[selective additional questions following consultation with Scottish Youth Parliament and third-party interest groups]	None
Income	Each adult and child	Wording amended from Family Resources Survey – sum / source / who received	Family Resources Survey (Poverty in GB) / Laeken Indicators (Poverty in EU)
Area satisfaction	Survey adult	[selective incorporation of existing questions from the existing Scottish Household Survey]	Scottish Household Survey 1999–2006

These principles would ensure that local authorities in Scotland have a first-class resource for monitoring poverty and social inclusion. However, despite the clear advantages of this over current approaches, the use of the Scottish Household Survey would still be limited for specialist populations and small local areas within local authorities. For example, it is unlikely that it would generate a sufficient sample to make robust comment on the levels of poverty among the estimated 1,000 immigrants who are entering Scotland each month since the barriers to working across the EU were removed in April 2006.[14] Likewise, insufficient data would be available to comment on the levels of poverty within each of the 22 rural service priority areas identified by the Scottish Executive as part of the *Closing the Opportunity Gap* programme. While it would be unreasonable to charge the Scottish Executive with the responsibility for measuring levels of poverty among every conceivable interest group, it would be both feasible and desirable to facilitate robust sub-population analysis by generating a toolkit to enable interest groups to conduct their own analyses of poverty by replicating the core measures now being proposed for the Scottish Hosuehold Survey and, thereafter, comparing their findings against the national benchmark of the Survey.

We conclude by suggesting a possible survey schedule for a 'Poverty and Social Inclusion' module in the Scottish Household Survey. This is intended to open debate with a view towards providing a first-class resource for measuring, understanding and tackling poverty and social inclusion in Scotland.

Notes

1 Scottish Executive, *Closing the Opportunity Gap*, 2006
2 This was discussed at length in the last independent review of the Scottish Household Survey – E McCaig, *Scottish Household Survey Review 2005*, 2005
3 A Knops, *Poverty Data, Anti-Poverty Strategy and Scottish Devolution*, Scottish Poverty Information Unit, 1998, p1
4 See note 3
5 Although Hirsch suggests that this reduction is not quite at the rate envisaged by the UK Government and that government intervention needs to be extended to meet the 2020 targets – D Hirsch, *What Will It Take To End Child Poverty? Firing on all cylinders*, Joseph Rowntree Foundation, 2006
6 ISER, 'Scottish and Welsh Extension Samples', *British Household Panel Survey*, 2006, Office for National Statistics, 2006
7 M Rowland and R Gatward, *Family Resources Survey 2001*, ONS, 2001, p4
8 Department for Work and Pensions, *Measuring Child Poverty*, 2003
9 J Bell and others, *Comparative Similarities and Differences between Action Research, Participative Research, and Participatory Action Research*, Critical Inquiry Seminar, Boga, Antioch University Seattle, 2004, available online at: http://www.arlecchino.org/ildottore/mwsd/group2final-comparison.html
10 I Dennis and A-C Guio, 'Poverty and Social Exclusion in the EU', *Statistics in Focus. Population and Social Conditions*, Eurostat, 2004
11 Although differences between different age stages (children, working age and pensioners) are reported, these are presented for Scotland, promoting an understanding that the incidence of poverty for these groups is uniform across Scotland.
12 See note 2; G Raab, C MacDonald and C MacIntyre, *Comparison of Income Data between Surveys of Scottish Households*, Napier University, 2005
13 See note 2
14 Citizens Advice Scotland, *Migrant Workers*, Briefing Paper, 2006